THE WRITER'S BOOK OF MATCHES

1,001 PROMPTS TO IGNITE YOUR FICTION

the staff of fresh
boiled peanuts,
a literary journal

WRITER'S DIGEST BOOKS
Cincinnati, Ohio
www.writersdigest.com

Visit our Web site at www.writersdigest.com for information on more resources for writers.

To receive a free weekly e-mail newsletter delivering tips and updates about writing and about Writer's Digest products, register directly at our Web site at http://newsletters.fwpublications.com.

09 08 07 06 05   5 4 3 2 1

Distributed in Canada by Fraser Direct, 100 Armstrong Avenue, Georgetown, ON, Canada L7G 5S4, Tel: (905) 877-4411. Distributed in the U.K. and Europe by David & Charles, Brunel House, Newton Abbot, Devon, TQ12 4PU, England, Tel: (+44) 1626 323200, Fax: (+44) 1626 323319, E-mail: mail@davidandcharles.co.uk. Distributed in Australia by Capricorn Link, P.O. Box 704, S. Windsor NSW, 2756 Australia, Tel: (02) 4577-3555.

Library of Congress Cataloging-in-Publication Data
The writer's book of matches : 1,001 prompts to ignite your fiction / by the editors of Fresh Boiled Peanuts (a literary journal).-- 1st ed.
        p. cm.
    ISBN 1-58297-411-X (alk. paper)
    1. Fiction--Authorship. 2. Literature--Stories, plots, etc. I. Fresh boiled peanuts.
    PN3378.W75 2005
    808.3--dc22

2005010799

Edited by
MICHELLE RUBERG

Designed & illustrated by
GRACE RING

Production coordinated by
ROBIN RICHIE

fw
F+W PUBLICATIONS, INC.

About Fresh Boiled Peanuts

The literary magazine *Fresh Boiled Peanuts* was born in March 2004. The staff is comprised of writers, editors, and other publishing insiders, whose goal is to discover and celebrate great new writers and their work.

To find out more about *Fresh Boiled Peanuts*, or to submit your own work for possible publication, check out the official *FBP* Web site at www.freshboiledpeanuts.com.

Staff members involved in the creation of this book include:

SCOTT FRANCIS
STEVE KOENIG
SUZANNE LUCAS
ALICE POPE
PHIL SEXTON

TABLE OF CONTENTS

INTRODUCTION

Stories start with an idea. And if you're a writer, or aspire to be one, ideas have to start with you. Sounds obvious, right? But what do you do when there are no ideas to be found? We, the editors at *Fresh Boiled Peanuts*, feel your pain. We've been there.

We're the first to admit that there's no magic recipe or scientific formula for creating ideas. And when you're plagued by fatigue, burnout, apathy, or writer's block, coming up with good ideas is even tougher*. Unfortunately, you can't just wait for inspiration. If you want to be a writer—*really* want to be a writer—you have to make it happen.

That's where *The Writer's Book of Matches* comes in. It's been designed to function as both muse and exercise partner. To that end, you'll find over one thousand writing prompts inside: moments of

* You can find bad ideas pretty much anywhere, but who wants those? Well, okay, there are a few authors I can think of, but let's not name names....

conflict, snippets of dialogue, or brief descriptions of unusual situations. Consider each one a "match," a handy little tool whose sole purpose is to ignite an idea that turns into a pleasant, possibly roaring, literary fire. Before attempting to work with any of them, however, be sure to read the "How to Use This Book" section that follows. It provides detailed insights into the various types of prompts and how they're meant to work, plus guidelines for using them to achieve different results—including breaking through writer's block.

Certain prompts may inspire you to write a single page. Others might grow into a short story—even a novel or screenplay. Don't limit yourself. Take each prompt as far as it will go. The goal is to have fun. Hone your craft. Be productive.

As sometimes happens, of course, you may not like what you've written. In this instance, look back over your work intent on finding something of value. We say this up front because all too often writers throw out the baby with the bathwater (and also because some of you are going to skip the "How to Use This Book section—you know who you are …). You may not like where your plot was headed, but perhaps you were in the process of creating a great character (even minor characters can be worth saving). In some cases, your true voice, rich with originality and spirit, will break through for a few lines. Or you'll create a wonderful exchange of dialogue. Make note of such discoveries before you throw anything away. Keeping them is a way of creating your own "book of matches," sparks for new stories you can work on down the road. These sparks will also encourage you to keep trying. They are signs that, yes, you are a writer, and that the more you write, the better your writing becomes.

Bottom line: Writing is cool. Being a writer is even cooler. And being a good writer makes you incredibly attractive to members of the opposite sex. Seriously. That's one of the reasons we stared the *Fresh Boiled Peanuts* journal—to celebrate writing and writers (not the sex part). After you've played with a few matches, come visit us at www.freshboiledpeanuts.com. We'd love to see your work.

HOW TO USE THIS BOOK

This book is packed with hundreds (and hundreds) of writing prompts, or "matches" as we like to call them. Light a match, you start a fire. Work with a prompt, you start a story. It can be the size of a candle flame (a single page) or grow into a raging inferno (a novel!). The point is that you're writing, regardless of how long any particular piece may turn out.

And while *The Writer's Book of Matches* is designed to help you start writing, even when you're stuck for inspiration, what we really want is to help you to start writing **EVERY SINGLE DAY**. Why is that so important? Because one of the most difficult things for a writer to do is actually sit down and write. You know that, otherwise you wouldn't be reading this book. Some writers are so proficient at avoiding the act of writing you almost have to admire them. Almost.

So here's the deal: Promise yourself, your spouse, your boss, your shrink—somebody you'll feel bad about letting down—that you're going to work with one of these prompts every day. If you don't feel like writing on Tuesday, get over it. Tuesday is a great day for writing. In fact, try your hand at two prompts on Tuesday. There's nothing good on television anyway. By doing this, you'll soon develop a writing habit. You'll feel weird if you miss a day, as if you've left important business unfinished. And there's a big side benefit. In *The Writer's Book of Wisdom*, Steven Taylor Goldsberry sums it up nicely:

> "If you wait to be inspired before you start writing, if you wait to experience that bolt of soul-clarifying insight, you're a fool and have no business being a writer. Write. The physical act itself will free the imagination. In this sense writing is like dancing, or sports, where the expression of grace comes only through movement."

So write everyday. Use a prompt as often as necessary to get yourself started. Eventually you will have trained your brain to come up with ideas at will—ideas worth writing about and, of equal importance, ideas worth reading about.

THREE TYPES OF PROMPTS

The Writer's Book of Matches provides three types of prompts. You won't find any that instruct you to "write about your favorite relative" or "write about the last time you cried." Our prompts tend to follow Goldsberry's rule: "Start where the story gets interesting."

To that end, each prompt details a conflict, revelation or unusual situation. In many cases, the protagonist seems obvious. In others, you'll have to do a little creative thinking. Also keep in mind that there are no "rules" here. If a prompt about a lonely housewife who decides to have an affair inspires you to write a story about the human invasion of Jupiter's tenth moon, more power to you!

One other note: Some prompts are brief. Don't assume that this means you won't have enough to write about. Our intent isn't to provide you with all of the details, only a direction in which to explore. In *Bird by Bird*, Anne Lamott uses a quote from E.L. Doctorow to describe this aspect of writing: "Writing ... is like driving a car at night. You can see only as far as your headlights, but you can make the whole trip that way."

The first—and most common—prompt is called a **SITUATION PROMPT**. Situation prompts provide an obvious protagonist who finds himself (or herself) in an unusual or emotionally charged situation. Sometimes, we designate the protagonist as "you," meant to suggest that you write about the prompt from second-person point of view. You don't have to do this, of course, and should feel free to write in second or third person, whichever you prefer.

In many cases, we liken the moment at which a situation occurs to a "plot point," defined by Syd Field in his classic book *Screenplay* as "an incident or event that 'hooks' into the action and spins it around in another direction." Here's an example:

> Upon reading the contents of his teenage stepdaughter's diary, a man is left fearing for his life.

In this instance, the protagonist is obvious, i.e., the man. Ask yourself who this man is. Think about what kind of relationship he has with his stepdaughter (keeping in mind, of course, that the relationship as he understands it might be totally different from her perception of it). Think about how he found the diary. Was he looking for it? Did she leave it out for him to find? Also, think about less obvious scenarios. Perhaps the man's wife forged an entry in the diary and left it for him to find. Why? Well, that's an interesting question. Sounds like a story worth telling, wouldn't you agree?

One thing that makes situation prompts so enjoyable is that they challenge you to come up with an intriguing spin on what might otherwise be a straightforward story. In other cases, you'll be presented with an intriguing situation (absurd, even) that you have to make believable. For example:

A dairy worker develops the uncanny ability to communicate telepathically with livestock.

Bizarre, certainly, but think of the implications. How would such a situation play out? How would it affect the protagonist? How could it affect the world in which the protagonist lives? How would the cows react? Should one of the cows be your protagonist? Now think about the various genres in which you could explore this prompt. Science fiction, social commentary, absurdist humor—any is fair game. Don't assume that the most obvious approach to telling a story is the best.

DIALOGUE PROMPTS are a little trickier. In a dialogue prompt you'll be given minimal information about the speaker and the person to whom they are speaking. In fact, you'll have to create the context in which the dialogue is being spoken. This gives you more freedom to create a plot, while at the same time forcing you to deal with character interaction before anything else. Here's an example:

> "He told me it was my fault, slammed the door, and took off. That was three days ago."

Use whatever dialogue you are given to help create a plot point or story situation. In the case of the prompt above, ask yourself who the speaker is. Are they male or female? What actions led to this statement and why? How will the situation be resolved? What will the speaker do next? How will the person being spoken to respond, and how will that affect the original speaker?

Approach dialogue prompts with the same imagination you would a situation prompt. There are no rules. Your speaker can be the president of the United States or a twelve-year old child. Your choice will greatly alter the landscape in which your story takes place, and may require you to do a bit more thinking before setting pen to paper (or fingers to keyboard, as the case may be).

Finally, be on the lookout for **ASSIGNMENT PROMPTS**. These are rare and can require extra effort on your part. They present a shared context in which multiple characters find themselves. Your job is to create a situation or conflict for each character given the context. Here's an example:

In the near future, women begin to out earn men by 50 percent. Write about how such conditions affect the following characters:
  • an ambitious young man who just recently married

- a young girl whose father is a stay-at-home dad
- an old man who pines for "the good old days"

If one of these options particularly strikes your fancy, then write as much as you can about that character. We suggest, however, trying to write at least a page for each character noted, as doing so will help you to think about the same story from multiple viewpoints. This is an invaluable exercise for learning how to write interesting secondary or minor characters (a great weakness with many writers—particularly scriptwriters).

GET INSPIRED

The simplest way to use these prompts is for instant inspiration. When you're in need of an idea, simply flip through the pages. The prompts aren't organized by topic or theme in the hopes that you'll find something useful on every page, no matter your area of interest. Search through the prompts until you come across one you find particularly interesting. Once you've found what seems like a winner, stop. That's right: stop. Think about the prompt for a minute before charging ahead. In many cases, you'll need to create a protagonist. It's important to do so with care, otherwise you may find yourself bored with a character dashed out without the proper forethought.

If you find yourself running out of steam after a page or two (or even a paragraph, for that matter), go ahead and switch to a new prompt. Eventually you'll discover one that gets your creative fires burning. And you needn't worry about running out of prompts—we've come up with some tricks that guarantee this book retains its usefulness for years to come (see the appendix for details).

GET REFRESHED

Try using prompts the same way you would a sorbet—as a palette cleanser between courses. If you've just finished writing a short story or something longer and you're feeling uninspired, pick out a prompt that interests you and write about it. What you write can be brief—a page will do. Set it aside for a day or two. Now go back and read what you wrote. You may discover that the story is intriguing enough to take further. Or, you may find yourself thinking about new projects. Fine. Start working on those. The point is to use as many prompts as needed to give your brain time to relax with a project that doesn't demand such intense focus, yet enables you to keep your writing "muscles" in peak condition.

In *The Writer's Idea Book*, Jack Heffron suggests using writing prompts for a different, yet equally sensible purpose:

> "If you are writing a piece you hope to publish, you may have trouble getting started for fear of making a mistake or writing something that isn't good. Trying too hard can freeze your imagination. The writing is stiff and clumsy. The ideas don't make sense or hold together. You many grow so frustrated that you stop writing before you've had a chance to get started.

"To move past these chilly moments, begin by writing on a less demanding piece … then, when the words begin to flow, switch to the piece you want to write."

And in his wonderful book *On Writing*, Stephen King suggests one more use for writing prompts. Once you've finished a project, put it away for a time before attempting a rewrite. Don't think about it. Write something else, in fact: "Something shorter, preferably, and something that's a complete change of direction and pace from your newly finished book." Doing so will help put distance between you and your original work, making the rewriting process that much easier.

Ultimately, whether you need to clear some creative mental space between projects or set the stage for attempting a larger, more involved piece, writing prompts enable you to go back to your "real" work more refreshed, energized and confident.

GET THROUGH WRITER'S BLOCK

There are a wide variety of beliefs about writer's block. In *Outwitting Writer's Block*, Jenna Glatzer blames "a noisy inner critic (or an even noisier next door neighbor), a story that you won't allow to come out and play, troubling life circumstances, insomnia, or myriad other things thrown in your path. ..." In *Beginnings, Middles & Ends*, Nancy Kress includes "fear of failure, fear of success, literary fogginess, and wrong direction" as causes. Some writers are less forgiving, including James V. Smith Jr. In *Fiction Writer's Brainstormer*, he states:

> "I think you have overindulged yourself on a steady diet of baloney for far too long. Why do writers think they have the privilege of a special dispensation for not working? What is this mysterious white lie known as writer's block? Face it—if you're not writing, it can only be because you're too lazy or you don't know what you are doing."

Ouch.

None of these statements help eliminate the problem, of course. And there are as many suggestions for breaking through writer's block as there are theories about what causes it.

We suggest that you think of writer's block as something other than an actual barrier to success (an idea that tends to make the problem more intimidating than it is). Try defining it as the absence of inspiration. Perhaps you've grown bored with your protagonist. Perhaps your plot has led to a dead end. Whatever the cause, getting back on track could be as simple as tapping into the same inspiration that drove you to write the story in the first place.

How? Look at your plot from a different angle. Reexamine your protagonist through the eyes of another character. In short, rediscover what makes your story interesting by stepping away from the path that's brought you to the point of writer's block and look at each element from a different perspective.

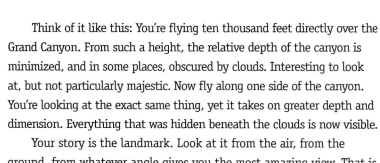

Think of it like this: You're flying ten thousand feet directly over the Grand Canyon. From such a height, the relative depth of the canyon is minimized, and in some places, obscured by clouds. Interesting to look at, but not particularly majestic. Now fly along one side of the canyon. You're looking at the exact same thing, yet it takes on greater depth and dimension. Everything that was hidden beneath the clouds is now visible.

Your story is the landmark. Look at it from the air, from the ground, from whatever angle gives you the most amazing view. That is how you rediscover your enthusiasm and inspiration. Learning how to look at your story in this way, however, can be tricky. And that's where writing prompts can be of use. Try the following exercise:

Pick a prompt at random. If it doesn't immediately lead you into a story, fine. If it's a prompt you've already used, it doesn't matter. Write about it anyway, with a different take on it than you had the first time. And write it with care. Craft your words, don't let yourself rip through a page or two and then say "Ha! That wasn't so hard." You're looking for a challenge. Use difficult prompts or ones that don't fully engage you. Force your imagination to work. Don't let yourself move on to an easier, more accessible prompt. Sweat a little. It'll be good for you. Work with the prompt until you find an approach that interests you. It doesn't have to be the obvious route. That's the point. By taking on a prompt you have no choice about, you're more likely to look at it from unexpected angles and figure out how to make it work. Here's an example:

> In the wee hours of every morning, a night watchman spends his time composing the symphony he's always dreamed of.

Maybe this prompt doesn't inspire you. Maybe, at first glance, you don't care about this night watchman. Fine—but you still have to create a story out of this prompt. That's the deal. So find the angle that does excite you. Maybe the owner of the building finds out what his night watchman is doing, decides he doesn't like it, and fires the poor guy (we'll call him "Mike"). Now maybe that's an angle you can write about: an out-of-work man who dreams of making the world take notice of him. Or maybe you write about the owner and how firing the night watchman affects others in the building. Do they protest because poor old Mike was told to hit the streets? Keep looking until you find an approach that excites you.

Make yourself write at least five hundred words inspired by this take on the prompt, then review what you wrote. Acknowledge the things you like, be it a character, a line of dialogue, whatever. By forcing yourself to find an interesting angle on any situation or character, you'll learn how to take any "problem" and turn it into an opportunity to rediscover what's so cool about your story.

Do this exercise enough times and the ability to look at any aspect of your work from a different point of view will become instinctual. You'll uncover fascinating details and intriguing concepts previously hidden from view, renewing and reenergizing your story in the process.

NOW STOP READING AND START WRITING

As we said before, write at least a prompt a day. It doesn't have to be much. You shouldn't feel like you've wasted a perfectly good prompt if you only write a paragraph. The point is to create a writing habit. It's like going to the gym. The more you go, the easier it is to keep going. And the more you work out, the better the results. Writing is no different. Work the muscle. Grunt and sweat if you have to, but work it. Not having an idea is no longer an option.

PROMPTS

"Well, if you could accuse anybody of being downright evil, it would be him."

A flight attendant learns that one of the passengers has brought a weapon on board.

A woman buys a gun for home defense, but two days later she can't find it.

"He's the cutest little boy. Makes it that much sadder, doesn't it?"

During his third night out of town, a traveling businessman discovers a voodoo doll in his hotel room.

A priest is attacked for being a pedophile. He is innocent of the crime but guilty of something far worse.

"Look, somebody has got to make a decision."

A married couple sets out on a six-month adventure, living on their boat while sailing from port city to port city.

"You know, they invented a word for guys like him."

A dentist is stabbed while he waits in line at the movies.

"I'm never doing that again."

During her first trip to Las Vegas, a woman experiences the luckiest night of her life.

"I just had the weirdest dream about you."

You accidentally overhear a conversation between two people you've never met. The topic of the conversation shocks and dismays you. Write about these conversations and describe how you respond to the content:

- a conversation between two stockbrokers
- a conversation between a priest and a member of his parish
- a conversation between a woman and the man with whom she's been cheating on her husband

"He was pretty religious once."

A man is given the ability to go back in time and change one event in his life.

Four college bandmates who haven't seen each other in years travel back to their former campus for a reunion.

A high-priced prostitute suspects that one of her best customers is falling in love with her.

"Time out! Time out! We can call that, right?"

A man ducks into a dress shop to escape a sudden downpour and finds himself in the middle of a heated debate between the employees.

Two skiers, one from America and one from France, get stuck together on a ski lift in the Swiss Alps.

A young couple embarks upon their very first home-improvement project together.

A woman whose husband is killed during a tour of duty overseas decides to turn her home into a boarding house.

A MAN ASPIRING TO BE A PRO BOWLER LOSES TO HIS YOUNG DAUGHTER.

A woman who's constantly quoting classic novels meets a literature professor at a cocktail party.

"I knew it was a mistake the moment it was over."

A young man works his way into an apprenticeship with a slick salesman.

"You don't have enough points, sir."

An architect is informed that his current project bears an uncanny resemblance to a "haunted" hotel destroyed decades earlier.

"I'll have an egg-white omelet and a side of sausage. And a beer, if you've got one."

While digging in a cereal box for the toy surprise, a child makes a grisly discovery.

A young anorexic woman is confronted by her supervisor about the issue.

A boy and his father awaken early to watch the sunrise from their mountain campsite, but they begin to panic when the sky remains dark long into the afternoon.

"I saw a picture of him on the Internet. Pretty scary."

"The only thing I've got left is my pride."

A writer's computer begins to flash messages on its screen, as if trying to communicate.

After thirteen years, a missing child is returned to her parents. The weird thing is ... she hasn't aged a day.

"Well, he said he was pretty drunk at the time."

An aviophobe sets out to win the respect of his disappointed pilot father.

Despite her current appearance, and the fact that she was in police custody, he knew she was the one.

"SERIOUSLY, IF THIS WERE THE WILD WEST, WE'D CALL HIM TRIGGER HAPPY."

"Stop thinking about how much you love him and start thinking about how much he hurts you."

A woman becomes frightened when she notices that her two-month-old baby is growing what appear to be fangs.

"You know how sand in an hourglass seems to flow faster as the amount in the top half decreases? That's what my life feels like."

Faced with poverty, a retired exotic dancer concocts a plan to take Broadway by storm.

A private investigator is asked to look into the disappearance of a stash of love letters sent to a widow by her husband when they were young.

I always start writing with a clean piece of paper and a dirty mind.

—Patrick Dennis

A parapsychologist and a holy man are called in to investigate an incident of spontaneous combustion. Just prior to the incident, the victim began speaking in tongues.

In the wee hours of every morning, a night watchman spends his time composing the symphony he's always dreamed of.

"What time is the next train?"

"Melba? Like the toast?"

A man suspects that his wife is having an affair. He secretly takes off work and follows her throughout the week.

"Gee, let me guess. You're not authorized to be in here, are you?"

A reporter uncovers the illegal activities of a local philanthropist. If he exposes these activities, however, many of the philanthropist's much-needed local charities will suffer.

After witnessing a terrible car wreck, a young man must confront the buried childhood memories of his own parents' demise.

"Every time I think I'm making progress—wham!—life kicks my legs out from under me."

A frustrated artist finds himself temporarily inspired after committing an act of violence.

"There are several possible answers to that question."

You just discovered that your friend has a very unusual, very dangerous hobby.

An ant decides to take his revenge upon the man who stepped on his family.

Upon reading the contents of his teenage stepdaughter's diary, a man is left fearing for his life.

A man in a hospital bed finds himself paralyzed from the neck down with no memory of his past.

You're secretly in love with your best friend's wife, and you suspect she feels the same way.

A mail carrier begins to suspect that a customer on his route is engaged in something fishy.

"Tell me what happened right before the crash, ma'am."

A WOMAN WAKES UP TO FIND HERSELF HORRIBLY DISFIGURED AFTER SPLURGING ON AN EXPENSIVE FACE CREAM THAT PROMISED "AMAZING RESULTS."

A woman is shopping in a busy grocery store when the roof collapses.

A woman comes home from work to discover her husband dead on the floor. Nothing in the house has been disturbed or taken. The only thing missing, in fact, is the man's wedding ring.

"He told me it was my fault, slammed the door, and took off. That was three days ago."

While in the post office buying stamps, a woman sees a picture of her estranged father on a Most Wanted poster.

"Please don't take this the wrong way, but I have to tell you something that's been bothering me."

A single father returns home to find an eviction notice hanging on his apartment door.

A botanist proves that plants feel pain and exhibit conscious thought.

A teenage girl is invited to her first sleepover.

A man takes his ten-year-old son on his first deer hunt.

The mother of three teens discovers that someone has stolen money from the "lunch-money jar."

A surfer trains to conquer the waves that killed his best friend.

"Your life isn't worth a damn to me."

Eight people sit in a boardroom waiting for their supervisor to arrive. When he does, he pulls out a gun, shoots one of the employees, and then himself.

"Look what I found in the dumpster!"

"I do *not* hate you."

After an old woman dies, her entire family fights over her meager belongings. Write how this affects the following witnesses/participants:
- her seven-year-old grandchild
- a police officer who arrives on the scene
- her oldest son, who was recently released from prison

"I lie awake at night thinking that marrying her was the wrong choice."

A disenchanted youth sets out on a cross-country trip in a last-ditch attempt to avoid following in the ill-fated footsteps of his professional wrestler father.

"When's the soonest you can get it too me? I've got to have the part as soon as possible."

I put the words down and push them a bit.
—Evelyn Waugh

Fresh out of college, you roll into a new town to start what you think is your dream job.

Your friend, who's having a mid-life crisis, begins to act dangerously impulsive.

"In all my time as a doctor, I've never seen this before. I'm at a loss."

A middle-class teenager attending an exclusive prep school on a scholarship struggles to fit in and impress the oh-so-hot captain of the lacrosse team who won't give her the time of day.

"I heard milk does a body good, but damn, girl, how much milk have you been drinking?"

A rabbi's daughter, who has devoted her life to the faith, begins to doubt the existence of God.

"I ask you, what's wrong with this picture?"

After five years of admiring her around the office, Michael finally gets the chance to make his move.

"How am I supposed to go to the bathroom?"

A harried twenty-something woman must contend with her overly demanding boss, her nagging mother who wants to be a grandmother, and her clingy ex-boyfriend who still wants to be friends.

A gambler at a private high stakes poker game is caught cheating.

A young girl sees a blue lion walk past her bedroom window and disappear into the nearby woods.

"Why do you have ten cans of Easy Cheese in your cart?"

A teenage girl's dead grandmother starts appearing in her dreams and revealing family secrets.

"When I took the lid off the shoebox, there was more cash than I had ever seen before."

A farmer dreams of fame and fortune after finding that his crops have grown to gigantic proportions overnight.

"It's not the dress. It's the woman who wears it."

"Well, to be honest, I threw it away."

A man gets out of bed one morning and discovers that he's a foot shorter than the day before.

"Funny, I always thought of myself as a ladies man."

It is for this, partly, that I write. How can I know what I think unless I see what I write?

—Erica Jong

BELIEVING THE FLOATING LIGHTS IN
HIS BACKYARD TO BE FIREFLIES,
A YOUNG BOY ACCIDENTALLY TRAPS
A FAIRY IN A MASON JAR.

44

A man is astonished to discover that he is growing gills.

An accountant believes that his "sick" co-worker has been killed by her husband.

A retired performance artist turned small-town grocer is convinced to participate in the local variety show. Dismayed at the town's lack of sophistication, he decides to give them a show they'll never forget.

"I just sat there and watched as his heart slowed down, then stopped."

Upon returning to his vessel, the first man to set foot on Mars discovers a strange, yet beautiful insect on the sleeve of his spacesuit.

"I ran farther and farther every day. But I never did get out of that town. Not really."

A woman finds her husband lying on the bathroom floor bleeding from his ear.

After suffering a terrible accident on his grandfather's farm, an unpopular boy must return to school with a hook for a hand.

While vacationing at a dude ranch, a wealthy business tycoon's daughter falls in love with a young cowboy.

As he sits before a detonator deciding which wire to cut, a bomb squad agent's life flashes before his eyes.

"You won't believe what I just got in the mail."

A midwife goes to the aid of a patient for what she hopes with will be an uneventful home birth.

"There's only one way out of this ..."

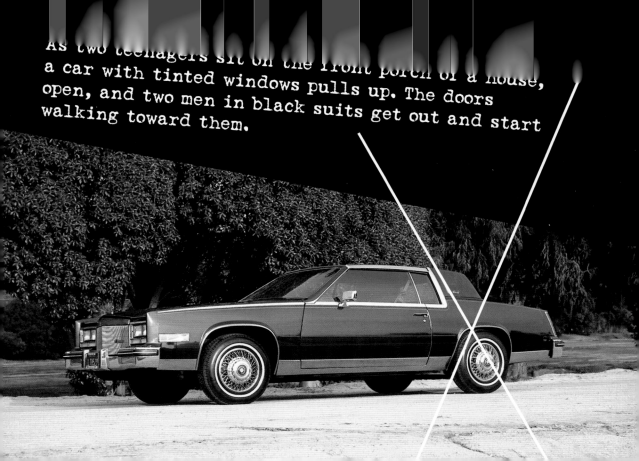

As two teenagers sit on the front porch of a house, a car with tinted windows pulls up. The doors open, and two men in black suits get out and start walking toward them.

"Okay, I think it's time to cut you off."

A woman looks out of her kitchen window to see a ball of fire rolling through her backyard.

Desperate for a new roommate, you place a personal ad in the paper. A number of interesting characters respond and request an interview. Write about your interviews with the following people and the subsequent results:

- a young female immigrant from the Ukraine
- a phone psychic who swears she has actual supernatural powers
- a professional bodybuilder
- a burnt-out college professor, recently retired from teaching

"Personally, I think they're a cult."

A depressed man has a brief, yet life-altering, encounter with a stranger.

A father and son are hiking when they are caught in the middle of a violent and unexpected snowstorm.

"He was the only man I ever loved. Could love, really."

After ten minutes, a phone sex professional realizes that she's been talking to her teenage son.

"Stay on this train until the end of the line."

After doing time for armed robbery, a young man looks for a new job—and a new life.

A woman overhears her boss's plans to let her go.

"Sometimes when I dream, it feels like there's someone else in there with me."

A mother discovers that her disabled son is selling drugs at school.

Two teenagers are rowing across a lake when they discover an artificial leg and a clown suit floating in the water.

"Thor would cream Superman easy, 'cause he's got that magic hammer."

Having never received a donation from the town's most successful lawyer, the head of a local charity decides to give the man a call and ask for a contribution.

A man sits on a bench quietly watching children play in the park.

An attractive woman becomes obsessed with her imperceptible flaws.

An eight-year-old boy pushes his mother down the stairs.

51

"I've got a bad feeling about it this time."

On the same day and at the same time, bombs explode in twelve different locations across the country.

"I know you can't walk; that's why I brought you this."

A reserved old woman decides that she wants to learn how to dance.

Three friends quit their high-paying jobs to find the fountain of youth.

"Love is not what I'm looking for right now. In fact, I'm happier without it."

An imprisoned man teaches himself how to paint.

While on a camping trip, a little boy strays from his family and happens upon a carnival in the middle of nowhere.

AFTER ONE TOO MANY COSMOS, YOU VOW TO YOUR TWO BEST FRIENDS THAT YOU'LL ASK OUT THE NEXT GUY WHO WALKS BY.

"It's not nuclear physics, damn it, it's just us. It can't be this hard to figure out."

A young ethnic woman—long obligated to an arranged marriage—prepares to introduce her boyfriend to her conservative parents.

"I hate you for interfering."

A writer begins to lose her ability to discern between fantasy and reality.

An intern at an off-Broadway theater company has her eye on the lead actor, but the lead's understudy is determined to make her fall in love with him instead.

"She was my last chance."

A husband and wife quickly find themselves in reality television hell.

"I think you broke it."

Write while the heat is in you. ... The writer who postpones the recording of his thoughts uses an iron which has cooled to burn a hole with.
—Henry David Thoreau

"How did you get in here?"

The existence of extraterrestrials is proven when a group of astronauts receives a complex message. In it, the leader of an alien species explains how he and his people are about to leave their own dying world for Earth. How do the following earthlings react once the news is made public?

- the vice president of the United States, who has secretly always believed in the existence of extraterrestrials
- the astronaut who received the original message
- a religious leader who has always condemned the belief in extraterrestrial life
- William Shatner

"Why did you pretend not to see me?"

A woman comes to believe that her husband is possessed.

A bored woman accidentally kills her husband's dog when she jokingly throws a rock at him.

56

A teen—who is regularly abused by her stepfather—runs away to find her birth father, whom she hasn't seen in years.

"Look … I'm making eggs. There's no deeper meaning to anything I'm doing here. It's breakfast. Plain and simple."

"Okay, it's true. I believe in vampires. But I have proof, okay?"

"Honey, give me the ATM card."

A man driving from Cincinnati to Cleveland in the middle of a snowstorm spots someone walking along the side of the road.

A boxer accidentally kills his opponent.

A child finds a magic ring in a box of cereal.

An anthropologist stumbles across a previously unknown native tribe in the wilds of northern Canada.

"Go ahead, compare me to your life's work. Just once I'd like to know where I stand."

A bank teller realizes that the guns aimed at him by two robbers are fakes.

For reasons unknown, insects begin to grow progressively larger—and smarter.

Seven people board a small boat for a tour around the islands, but when the boat returns to the dock, only six people remain on board.

A man in Tokyo looks out of his window to see a cow walking down the street.

DUE TO THE RAVEN THAT FOLLOWS HIM WHEREVER HE GOES, A YOUNG MAN IS CONVINCED THAT SOMETHING TERRIBLE IS ABOUT TO HAPPEN.

A man, distraught over his pending divorce, finds himself walking aimlessly around a department store. He wanders into an employee break room, falls asleep, and gets locked in for the night.

"I'm not sure, but I think that suit is wearing you, and not the other way around."

Several children at a Catholic school witness a miracle.

"Ordinarily, I'd never agree to this sort of thing, but you've got an honest face."

A woman purchases an old cookbook in a used bookstore and discovers a note tucked inside its pages.

An eco-journalist investigates the reasons behind the rapid reduction in the population of a local bird species.

"I'd like
you to
come home
with me."

"Let's get this straight … I don't like your father. I've never liked your father, and there is no way that anyone, including you, will ever get me to like him. So why don't we just stop pretending that I do."

A woman embarks on a self-improvement project a few months before she's expected to attend her ex-husband's wedding.

An elderly couple awakens one morning to find all of their furniture mysteriously piled in the middle of the living room.

"How do you think it works?"

"It's not worth getting pushed down a flight of stairs for. I'm pretty sure of that much, anyway."

An old saying takes on new meaning when a woman sees, literally, "what the cat dragged in."

Hell
freezes
over.

A conservative politician, very much in bed with certain special interest groups, finds himself strongly attracted to the liberal director of a local homeless shelter.

"You might notice a foul odor."

After a night of heavy drinking, an eye surgeon makes a terrible mistake while performing an otherwise simple procedure.

Due to an unexpected power loss, a pilot must make an emergency landing in the middle of the ocean.

"This is all I have."

An alien lands on Earth and encounters humans for the very first time—at a cattle ranch in Texas.

The family pet, actually a rare breed of housecat, goes missing. Two days later, the owners receive a ransom note.

A little girl's imaginary friend starts giving her lucrative stock tips.

"You know, it doesn't take a detective to see that you've been screwing around behind her back."

Campers cower in fear as a man with a shotgun enters their campsite.

An artist loses her grasp on reality and becomes convinced that she's married to a well-known artist.

An afternoon joyride turns deadly when an innocent prank backfires.

A struggling actor is offered a well-paying role in a commercial about impotence.

"I just can't do this any-more!"

65

"I remember his birthday party like it was yesterday."

A poor young woman hits the lottery for thirty-four million dollars. As she runs across the street to tell her neighbors, a car hits her.

"Ten bucks says you can't go a week."

While on her deathbed, a mother tells her son that his real father is a famous celebrity.

You decide to join a gym, not so much to get in shape, but to find Mr. Right (or Mr. Right Now).

"Well ... if you cross Brad Pitt's looks with Gomer Pyle's voice, you're getting pretty close."

An escaped felon hides from the police within a group of homeless men.

"Oh, she killed her. I'm sure of it."

"I know kung fu."

A man overhears a conversation and misinterprets its meaning.

When I say "work" I only mean writing. Everything else is just odd jobs.
—Margaret Laurence

"I'll tell my grandchildren about you."

You are riding a crowded subway with a huge wad of cash in your inside coat pocket.

A young woman invites two friends to her family's old country house for a long weekend. She neglects to tell them there is no electricity.

A woman discovers that her new boyfriend is completely hairless.

A struggling rock band gets its first big break.

"Nah, I don't love her. But she's, you know, good where it counts."

Desperate for money, a retired stuntman volunteers to perform the most dangerous Hollywood stunt of his career.

A teenager finds out that his father was a priest and his mother a nun.

"I'm here to answer the ad in the paper."

After signing up to serve a term as a doctor for the Peace Corps, you discover that the reality of the situation you find yourself in is far worse than expected.

A middle-aged man receives an anonymous love letter.

"Sean Connery, of course. Roger Moore couldn't fight his way through a troop of Girl Scouts."

A woman experiences a major breakthrough during a therapy session.

"Seriously. I was eating at the same restaurant as him, and let me tell you, he didn't look like such a 'badass' to me."

A marine biologist discovers the washed up body of what appears to be the Loch Ness Monster. Write about how this discovery affects:
- a lifelong skeptic who has written several books denying the creature's existence
- a self-proclaimed monster hunter who has spent years searching for Nessie
- the lives of the people in a small town close to where the monster was found
- a young couple who happen to be vacationing near Loch Ness when the body is found

A hotel housekeeper finds a suicide victim in one of the rooms.

A woman awakens to find herself levitating above the bed.

DURING THE STATE FAIR OPENING CEREMONIES, A PRIZE-WINNING PIG IS KIDNAPPED.

God
decides
He needs
to take a
vacation.

Three neighborhood children watch quietly as a long black car rolls to a stop in front of an abandoned house.

A zookeeper arrives at work to find that three of the most valuable—and dangerous—animals in his area are missing.

While her husband is away on a business trip, a woman hears someone approach her front door and insert a key into the lock.

"It took him years to get back on the wagon, then three days later all the wheels fell off."

A group of salesmen on their way to a company retreat decide to stop and investigate a strange-looking suitcase on the side of the road.

"It seems funny to say something so cliché, but there has to be a reason why we keep meeting like this."

In any really good subject, one has only to probe deep enough to come to tears.
—Edith Wharton

"Sometimes I think I work so hard because I don't have anything else to do."

After fighting a ten-year battle with alcoholism, a man moves to Japan to study with a Zen philosopher.

A deadly virus is released in a heavily populated U.S. city, not by terrorists, but by the U.S. military.

"If we have this conversation, it's going to end badly for you. Consider that a fair warning."

A young woman dies in a car accident, and her grief-stricken parents are shocked by what they find while cleaning out her apartment.

"She checked out last night."

A father learns that his son has decided to pursue a career as a makeup artist.

74

Two convenience store employees are stuck at work during a blizzard.

A stay-at-home dad joins the neighborhood "mommies club."

While reading the front page of your local paper, you spot a picture of someone you know, and beneath it is a story that takes your breath away.

"Fine. You're the 'native.' You tell me how to find our way back."

While the baby naps, a nanny for a well-to-do couple begins nosing around her employers' desk drawers.

"I promised I wouldn't tell anyone, but I guess I can trust you."

Twenty-something women in a knitting club regularly share gossip and secrets with one another. Today, one of the women reveals a secret that leaves the others stunned.

"C'mon, let's try it. They test this stuff all the time to make sure it's safe."

"Promise me that you'll take care of my kids."

There's a new standard of beauty in Hollywood: Fat.

An upstanding citizen driving the speed limit is stopped by the police on his way to pick up his kids from school.

"Do you ever feel like you just haven't got the common sense that everyone else was born with?"

You and your lab partner are assigned to dissect a cadaver, and decide to investigate the background of the body.

A death row inmate, convicted for a crime he didn't commit, is asked to choose his last meal.

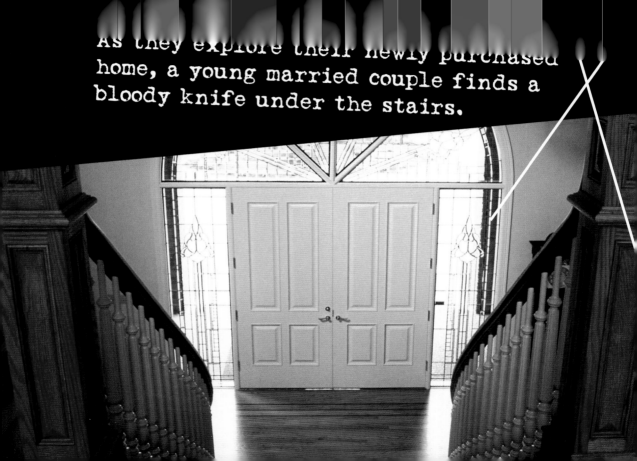

As they explore their newly purchased home, a young married couple finds a bloody knife under the stairs.

While traveling abroad, a nurse finds herself on a tour bus with an expectant mother who begins to go into labor.

"I'm sure that's an urban legend."

In the near future, women begin to out earn men by 50 percent. Write about how such conditions affect the following characters:
- an ambitious young man who just recently married
- a young girl whose father is a stay-at-home dad
- an old man who pines for "the good old days"

"If I had her confidence, I'd have made the move long ago."

A PR firm's newest client becomes a public relations nightmare.

"Either you give me a raise, or I quit!"

Making a decision to write was a lot like deciding to jump into a frozen lake.
—Maya Angelou

A young woman must run errands while wearing an embarrassing and inappropriate outfit.

While walking past his neighbor's house on garbage day, a man sees what looks like a human foot stuffed down in a trash can.

"Oh no. Don't blame her."

You return home from work to find your house totally empty.

A bartender begins an e-mail relationship after finding an address written on a dollar she received as a tip.

"Look, Chief, I don't know who the culprit is. But I can tell you that the whole damn box is empty."

"I'VE SEEN ENOUGH MONKEYS FOR ONE DAY, THANK YOU VERY MUCH."

Full of self-loathing that you attribute to your childhood, you begin to write a memoir.

Using only the money in his pocket, an up-and-coming young businessman accepts a wager to start a profitable business in less than a year.

A famous family moves in next door to you.

While driving to work one morning, you decide to pass the office and keep on driving.

Two writers have trouble deciding on the exact wording of their wedding vows. The groom is a journalist, the bride an academic.

"This is the most boring party I've even been to. Let's sneak out."

You arrive at your office to find that your personal belongings have been boxed up.

A couple's car breaks down while they're vacationing in a foreign country.

Over the course of one week, a rural woman notices that several items have disappeared from her clothesline.

"Thanks for seeing me. I need to discuss something important, and I didn't want to do it over the phone."

A gay man, who has not made his sexual orientation public, runs into several co-workers while on a date.

"Mom, Principal Burns is on the phone. He wants to talk to you."

Writing is a way of talking without being interrupted.
—Jules Renard

A journalist doing a story on what it's like to live on death row begins to fall for one of the inmates she's been interviewing.

"Back off, mister. I don't get paid enough to deal with these kinds of shenanigans."

What appears to be the fuselage of a strange aircraft is uncovered during the site excavation for a future strip mall.

"I got the best e-mail today!"

A nurse in a mental hospital discovers that a well-known missing person is being held there against her will.

A trash collector uncovers something extraordinary in the back of his truck.

"All I know is that one minute he's standing there talking about his favorite Merlot, the next he's on the floor in a pool of blood."

A TWELVE-YEAR-OLD BOY DECIDES TO BECOME A SUPERHERO.

A father of two is diagnosed with Lou Gehrig's Disease.

Two children get lost during a zoo field trip and find themselves trapped in an animal habitat.

A fraudulent psychic begins to experience real occult phenomena.

"I think you're out of options."

"Shut up, man. She'll hear you."

Two men argue on a street corner and a crowd gathers to watch. Write about the incident from the perspective of:
- one of the men involved in the argument
- an observer who happens upon the scene after the argument has started
- an observer who knows one of the two men

"If I didn't think you'd hit me back, I'd slap you for that."

Just a few days after getting married, a young newlywed becomes obsessed with building a time machine.

A young child begins to show sociopathic tendencies.

"I'm thirty-five and still single. You're twenty-six and divorced. So what are we doing wrong?"

The doorbell rings. You open it and find two packages on the porch—one large and one small.

"Are you following me?"

With no room for error, a mathematician must plot the course of a missile that will destroy a large earth-bound meteor.

You win a seat on the first commercial space shuttle flight.

The most durable thing in writing is style, and style is the most valuable investment a writer can make with his time.

—Raymond Chandler

"Move away from the leopard print. I repeat: Move away from the leopard print."

An old woman's pet parrot begins speaking in rhyming couplets.

Parents give their five-year-old a piece of paper and some crayons. Twenty minutes later he proudly shows off his nearly perfect reproduction of a famous painting.

A lonely woman wins a trip for two to a romantic destination. She approaches a complete stranger and offers him the other half of the prize.

"Put it down or I'll scream."

An ailing airline pilot must atone for the adulterous sins of his past to reconnect with his estranged children before it's too late.

"I wish I could describe her without sounding like an idiot."

After a near-death experience, a young man is haunted by visions of a beautiful yet terrifying afterlife.

A film student decides to make a documentary about the memories of his ailing grandfather.

While serving a long tour of duty overseas, a soldier becomes distraught that he can't remember his wife's face.

"So how long has this been going on and when were you planning on telling me about it?"

A teenager orders lunch from a fast food drive-thru and finds something odd in the bag.

A group of cavemen witnesses a strange light in the night sky.

A FAMILY MEMBER DISAPPEARS WHILE VACATIONING ON A CRUISE SHIP.

After the death of his grandfather, a young man goes through all that remains of the old man's possessions. One item—a lock box—is stuffed full of faded yellow letters. They are written in French, which is odd, as the young man's grandfather was Irish.

"I'd better practice my knife skills."

After being dumped a week before her would-have-been-lavish wedding, a woman decides to go on her honeymoon anyway, traveling alone to a swanky, tropical resort.

Hundreds of dolphins and whales begin to congregate all along the Pacific coast.

"Yeah, sure she's the strongest person I know. But she's still going to have to ask for help at some point."

Writing is manual labor of the mind: a job, like laying pipe.

—John Gregory Dunne

An alcoholic attends his first social event since leaving rehab.

Though paralyzed by his fear of heights, a man considers bungee jumping to impress someone.

"You know, on some days it's like I can see the whole 'divine plan' behind the universe. On others, I think the world was thrown together from whatever bits of trash the universe could spare."

In the middle of a long shower, a young woman suddenly realizes that she is no longer alone in her apartment.

A young married couple inherits a house that is rumored to be haunted. It is not, but the husband discovers that his wife is sexually aroused by the possibility.

"Mommy, I don't like this."

"It would be best if you put that back where you found it, sir."

94

A renowned psychic finds that her powers of precognition have vanished.

After forty years of living with a traveling carnival, the strong man and bearded lady retire and attempt to adjust to a normal life as a married couple.

A young woman who's just spent several hours studying at a coffeehouse notices someone watching her.

A well-dressed older man is sitting at a hotel bar holding a gold watch in one hand and a photograph in the other. He sighs deeply and nurses his drink.

"Lust. If my life were being written by Shakespeare, that would be my tragic flaw."

It is dis-
covered that
the pie in
a small-town
diner has
curative
properties.

After watching Eminem's movie *8 Mile*, a mild-mannered businessman is inspired to participate in a rap battle.

Suffering from a mid-life crisis, a fifty-year-old businessman quits his job and goes on a quest to "get the band back together."

"He was born that way, I guess."

America decides to invade North Korea due to evidence of weapons of mass destruction proliferation. The draft is reinstated in order to make this invasion possible. Write about how this news affects the following characters:
- a mother who lost a daughter in the war in Iraq
- a young man who turns eighteen in three months
- a newscaster gunning for a promotion

"I don't understand where all the self-loathing comes from."

When writing a novel a writer should create living people; people not characters. A character is a caricature.
—Ernest Hemingway

97

"If you can guess what I have in my pocket, you can have it."

A social worker spends her summer volunteering at the zoo and observing the social behavior of monkeys.

The storm of the century is coming— on your wedding day.

A traveling businessman throws his laptop out of the hotel room window.

"I'm giving you ten seconds. Then I swear I'll kick the door in."

While transporting a convict through a remote area, a prison van skids off the road and into a snow bank.

A boy falls into a cave when the ground in his backyard collapses.

"WHAT THE HELL DO YOU KNOW ABOUT ANYTHING? I MEAN, SERIOUSLY, YOU'RE JUST A DOG."

You see your brother, a recovering alcoholic, buying beer at a local store.

A carpenter discovers an important historic document while gutting an old farmhouse.

A philanthropist's plane crashes in the jungle, where the native tribe he has fought so hard to protect begins hunting him.

"I just want to hug him. I know it's the wrong time, the wrong place, but I don't care."

A young man learns that his girlfriend got pregnant and had an abortion without telling him.

The morning after a heavy snowfall, a single man sees a set of footprints leading away from his house.

After falling asleep on his shift, a prison guard awakens to find that all of the cells are empty.

"How do I look?"

While vacationing with his parents in France, a little boy finds an antique hand grenade in the middle of a field.

"Sixteen years, gone to hell."

Two boys decide to play tricks on their neighborhood after a recent string of bear attacks.

A man and his wife stop to investigate a disabled car on the side of the road.

"He's got a father, sure, but he'll always be a bastard to me."

Anybody can write a three-volume novel. It merely requires a complete ignorance of both life and literature.
—Oscar Wilde

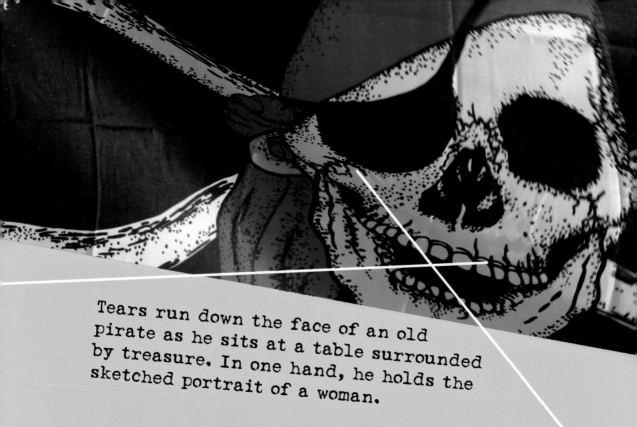

Tears run down the face of an old pirate as he sits at a table surrounded by treasure. In one hand, he holds the sketched portrait of a woman.

A suburban couple finds a handsome, young man asleep on their doormat.

"You haven't got a clue, have you?"

A couple on the brink of a nasty divorce get snowed in together during a blizzard.

The Ten Commandments are discovered in a previously unopened chamber in Machu Picchu.

After completing a solo camping trip, a woman gets her film developed and discovers that several of the photos are of her ... sleeping.

"I just want to quit my job and move someplace where nobody else knows me."

"Either you tell him, or I will."

"You smell terrible! What happened?"

While working on the air conditioning, a father finds some loose floorboards in his teenager's bedroom.

A man's doorbell rings. He looks through the peephole to see a figure wearing a yellow jumpsuit and a motorcycle helmet with wings painted on each side.

"I just wish ... the timing had been better."

A psychiatrist is offered a large sum of money to treat a patient, but he must first sign a contract stating that he will never reveal the patient's identity to anyone. If he does, the consequences will be severe.

Three boys decide to go have some fun at the local swimming hole. Shortly after they arrive, something terrible happens.

"At least I'm walking out of this alive."

After accepting a dare, a girl discovers that she has a fondness for eating live bugs.

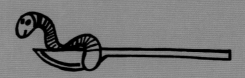

Ten young soldiers are assigned to a difficult mission in enemy territory. One of the soldiers believes that it is a suicide mission.

"I can't believe you've taken up jogging. What about our pact?"

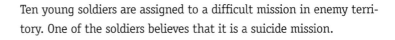

With his young son looking on, a mugger shoots and kills a man at a walk-up ATM. He then tells the boy that this is how strong men "survive." Ten years later, the son finds himself in a situation that proves his father wrong … or right.

A woman digging in her garden uncovers a sealed, ancient box.

"So they can't get the landing gear down and we were up there just circling for, like, three hours."

"Helpful hint: Wait until you're sober before trying that again."

An elderly woman decides to rebel against the conventions of socially acceptable behavior.

While hiding from police, a drug dealer is confronted by a man claiming to be God. In his attempt to make the stranger leave, the drug dealer accidentally kills him.

A man decides to ask his girlfriend of eight months to marry him. She replies, "What about your wife?"

"For the love of God, don't tell me that you *lost the freaking map*."

A young woman loses her ability to speak, save for one word.

A book comes and says, "Write me."

—Madeleine L'Engle

107

"Oh, I'll propose
a toast to the
happy couple,
all right."

In the middle of the night, a man rolls over just in time to see his wife pull on a pajama top. In the moonlight, he notices bruises on her arms that weren't there when they went to bed.

"Go ahead, butcher the language. Nobody cares anymore anyways."

An obese young man successfully sues the fast food industry.

A young girl awakes in the night to see a dark figure sitting next to her bed. When she turns on the light, the figure is gone.

"Love gets me into more trouble than hate ever could."

A Midwest farmer pauses as he hears the news: the United States has adopted the barter system.

A man believes himself to be possessed when his hand starts writing a message of its own volition.

A train travels from Paris to Rome. There are several interesting characters staying in the sleeping cars. Write about what happens to each of them during the night:

- an older married couple, trying to recapture the romance of their youth
- two young women who agree to share a car after it's announced there are no more rooms available
- a football goalie who, earlier that evening, gave up the winning goal to his team's greatest rivals

"It's always the quiet ones, you know?"

A young woman's suitor attempts to woo her by killing two pheasant and presenting them to her.

"You're a long way from home, boy."

AN ARTHRITIC VIOLINIST ATTEMPTS TO COMPOSE HER FINAL OPUS.

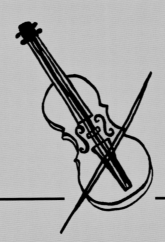

"I told you I'm allergic to shell- fish!"

Following the trail of several terrible murders, a London detective stumbles upon an unlikely clue when he makes an impulsive visit to Stonehenge.

Two high school sweethearts arrange to meet for a drink fifteen years after graduation.

"You have ten seconds ..."

While his wife is away at a company function, a man decides to surprise her by cleaning the house. In the process, he finds a passport hidden in the closet. The face on it is hers. The name is not.

A twenty-year-old with no extended family is told that his parents have been killed.

"Mom, you've got to stop dragging me into the middle of things."

Two cross-country skiers come across an isolated cabin. The front door is open, a hot meal is on the dining room table, and a car is in the driveway, but no one appears to be home.

"Have you noticed that he waits until you have an olive in your mouth, then he asks you a question?"

A housewife—and compulsive Internet shopaholic—contemplates having an affair with her hunky UPS man.

Three businessmen driving to a convention in Las Vegas get lost in the middle of the desert.

A man hears the voice of God speaking to him through his emergency short-wave radio.

A surgeon secretly feels responsible for the death of a patient.

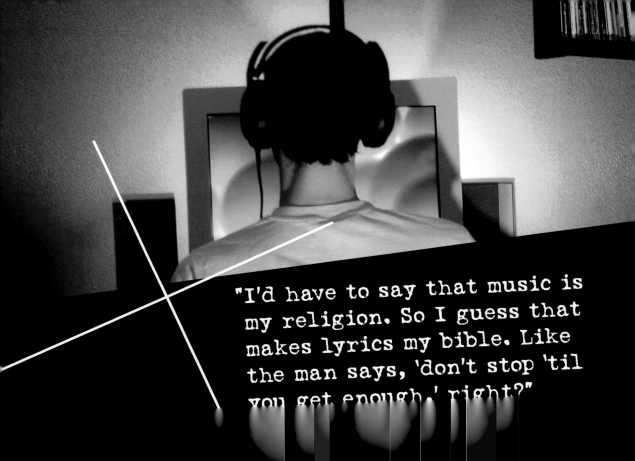

"I'd have to say that music is my religion. So I guess that makes lyrics my bible. Like the man says, 'don't stop 'til you get enough,' right?"

Two children come home to find a strange man asleep in their father's easy chair.

A woman finds a strange laptop computer set up in her living room. Beside it sits a handwritten list of instructions.

"I was just trying to stay out of the way. Good plan, huh?"

While on a cruise, a man and wife spot several dead whales beached along the coast.

A young scientist finds the cure for cancer. Just as he's about to report his discovery, he receives a menacing phone call warning him against it.

"When I watch her paint, I feel like I'm learning more about her than I ever could by talking with her."

A book is simply the container of an idea—like a bottle; what is inside the book is what matters.

—Angela Carter

115

While at the zoo with his father, a young boy notices a cage with bars that have been pried open.

An excommunicated priest receives a holy relic in the mail.

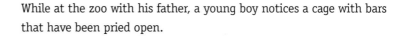

A vintage car enthusiast patrols the streets of his neighborhood during a rash of tire slashings.

"I'm sorry. Your position is being eliminated."

A father takes his young daughter shopping for her first bra.

"You ever notice how he talks like he's in a movie from the '40s?"

After his company folds due to scandal, a high-powered executive takes a job as a school bus driver.

"HE'S PRETTY SCARY LOOKING FOR A MIME."

A man looks out his window to see someone digging in his backyard.

A documentary filmmaker is in the process of capturing extraordinary footage of a sunken World War II destroyer when his submersible begins to lose buoyancy. Write about how this turn of events affects the following characters:
- the documentary filmmaker, who's finally found what he's spent years looking for, only to potentially die in the process
- the pilot of the underwater craft, who doesn't really care about the filmmaker's stupid boat
- the captain of the research vessel, floating far above the problem where he cannot help

While skipping school one day, two boys get stuck in an elevator with a pregnant woman.

A couple learns that their child is autistic.

"Bet me.
Please."

Nine months after running his yacht upon the reef surrounding a deserted island, an actor tries to stay "sane" by playing the roles of his friends and family.

"I just go on faith. I know it sounds naïve, but I really believe these things work out the way they're supposed to."

"Your mom is like Columbo, man. Get her in on this and that dude is nailed."

A pregnant mother of two learns that her army reserve husband has been killed by friendly fire while on duty in Iraq.

While looking through his recently deceased father's attic, a middle-aged man finds a box containing old newspaper clippings about an as yet unidentified serial rapist

A cowboy composes a letter at his favorite saloon before going out to face another gunfighter.

A doctor meets with a patient suffering from multiple personality disorder. These personalities switch unpredictably. They are a passenger of a cruise ship, Jesus, a ten-year-old girl, and a well-known television character.

An old man returns to the tree in which he carved the initials of his long lost childhood sweetheart.

"It got me to thinking: Am I as big a disappointment to him as he is to me?"

Halfway through surgery on an unidentified victim of rape and attempted murder, the head surgeon realizes that the patient is his daughter.

A former child star has an existential crisis as he watches reruns of his show on TV Land.

"She's in the backroom," he told the ambulance driver.

A high school teacher sits at his desk grading papers, wondering if his life has been wasted teaching such poor students.

"I jammed it in so hard, it got stuck in the bone. Do you know how hard it is to pull a knife out of bone?"

After dating for three months, a couple decides to spend the weekend at a secluded bed-and-breakfast.

A beekeeper must come to terms with his own guilt after his daughter is accidentally stung to death.

Angry with his parents, a young boy sneaks into the baggage compartment of a Greyhound bus, hoping to find freedom and adventure on the road.

"Hold onto something. This is gonna be wicked."

A middle-aged widow is having a secret affair with her best friend's college-age son.

"What do you mean you lost my reservation?"

Armed with a bottle of whisky and a two-by-four, a tough biker with good intentions sets out to deliver vigilante justice in a town gone bad.

After years of following dead end leads, a tabloid reporter stumbles across hard evidence of a legendary small town monster.

A young anorexic woman is confronted by her supervisor about the issue.

> Literature is the art of writing something that will be read twice.
>
> —Cyril Connolly

AN AMATEUR MAGICIAN RECEIVES A TELEPHONE CALL FROM THE FBI.

"If I could do it all over again, I would, and I'll tell you why."

A woman awakens from dental surgery with the terrifying belief that something terrible happened while she was unconscious.

After having a steel plate put in his head, a man begins to hear radio signals from another world.

A babysitter feels responsible when a small child dies in her care.

"This is my first time on a plane."

While flipping through a magazine, a woman recognizes a picture of herself in a section dedicated to fashion victims.

"Why waste your time trying to figure them out? I say stop worrying about it and enjoy yourself."

"I refuse to sign."

A bookstore clerk decides to recommend the same book to all customers, regardless of what they ask her.

"You would think that after twenty years, I'd know better."

A woman obsessed with Elvis sets off on a pilgrimage to visit Graceland.

A disgruntled maitre d' decides to exact vengeance on his pretentious, demanding customers.

After skiing for several days without incident, a young woman breaks her wrist while removing her boots in the lodge.

"I know you're not religious, but why don't you try praying anyway?"

A father tells his daughter a family secret that prompts her to tear up her college applications and purchase a one-way plane ticket.

A woman visiting a foreign country for the first time is astonished to realize she can speak the language.

"I ASSUME SINCE YOU'RE WEARING A RING THAT YOU MUST HAVE A PERKY LITTLE WIFE AT HOME, HMMM?"

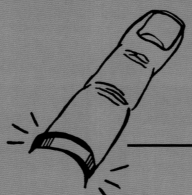

"Where on earth did you find that?"

A bus traveling through Mexico breaks down while passing through a small town. It will be ten hours before another bus passes through the area, forcing the passengers to explore the town. Write about this situation from the point of view of the following characters:
- an escaped convict trying to get as far away as possible from civilization
- a woman who is strongly attracted to the bus driver
- a teenager longing for an adventure

"I know it's terrible. But I kind of *like* hurting people."

A midget and his pet monkey are recruited for a special deep-space mission.

"Don't pretend to understand what I'm going through."

You find the Venus de Milo's arms.

A man and a woman who've been driving together for the past four days decide to take shelter under a bridge during a hailstorm.

Following the death of her outdoorsman husband, a woman embarks upon a hike along the Appalachian Trail.

A widow discovers a photograph of her husband in his early twenties, holding a baby that she doesn't recognize.

"Cliché as it sounds, that's when I realized I was gay."

If the writing is honest it cannot be separated from the man who wrote it.
—Tennessee Williams

While taking a stroll around the family farm, a boy and his grandfather stumble across a mysterious footprint. It visibly frightens the old man.

"It took all the willpower I could muster not to order the bowl of cheese soup again."

A woman learns that her beloved terrier is really a robot.

An orphaned boy discovers that the man who saved his life is the same man who caused the death of his parents.

"If you're looking for trouble, she just had her legs waxed."

While driving out west, a girl finds herself in the path of a stampeding herd of wild horses.

"Perfect. Now we're late *and* lost."

A man receives a package with no return address. It contains a pirate-style eye patch and a note.

A man visits a fortuneteller and is told he will die in one day.

A GUITARIST FOR AN ANARCHIST PUNK ROCK BAND MOONLIGHTS AS A GOVERNMENT OPERATIVE.

You find an envelope full of money in a parking lot and decide to spend it on an adventure.

A man, his lover, and his wife share a cab ride back to their hotel after an appearance on *The Jerry Springer Show*.

For $100,000, a woman in need of cash agrees to be the surrogate mother for a rich, childless couple.

A teacher informs his class that Santa Claus is black.

"It's not the women you're attracted to. It's the women you attract."

Two college engineering students invent something that could radically change the world.

"You read your spam?"

"Darn it, Amy, quit eating my pudding cups!"

You and your friends concoct a scheme to raise money for a cross-country trip to visit your girlfriend at college.

Disenchanted with the business world, an entrepreneur sets out to realize his boyhood dream of becoming an archaeologist.

A terribly overweight woman joins a salsa dancing class.

"Bless me, Father, for I have sinned; it's been fifteen years since my last confession."

A boy selling raffle tickets door to door stumbles upon a crime scene.

During a powerful tornado, a convict is thrown, unharmed, from his demolished jail cell into a ditch outside.

"Heads, we get married. Tails, we break up. How's that?"

A teenager learns that her father is going to re-marry. He also wants her to come stay with him and his new wife for the summer.

The year is 2200. Nearly 85 percent of the U.S. population is morbidly obese. Write about the following individuals living in such a culture:
- a slender young woman
- a plastic surgeon who injects fat into thin patients so they can fit the new "ideal"
- a child who sees photographs of his great-grandparents when they were young and thin

"Can you recommend a good book?"

In an attempt to win a pretty maid's affection, a young squire tries to impersonate the knight he serves.

"I'd walk across razors for you."

A man decides to attend the funeral of his favorite author.

"Do you notice anything different about me?"

A former police detective who lost everything after an unfortunate shooting
incident plots the perfect bank robbery.

A pre-teen scientific genius invents a special device that allows him
to control the minds of adults.

"I promised I wouldn't tell anyone, but I guess I can trust you."

A reality show contestant who can't handle the sudden fame retreats
to the woods to become a recluse.

A filmmaker captures an extraordinary improvisational performance on camera, but can't use it without ruining the career of the actor who gave it.

"I know it sounds corny, but this is really going to be the trip of a lifetime."

After trying for more than twenty years, a man finally solves the Rubik's Cube he got in high school.

When a murder weapon is checked for fingerprints, the only ones found correspond with those registered to the victim.

"Listen, man, we've been friends a very long time and I need to tell you something important."

While researching her family genealogy, a woman discovers that her grandfather was a Nazi prison guard during World War II.

"That homeless guy is staring at you again."

A window washer witnesses something horrifying while working outside a high-rise apartment building.

"Just pretend I'm not here."

An airport security line erupts in violence.

After suffering millions of casualties during a military conflict, the U.S. government passes a law that every woman over the age of twenty-one must produce at least one male child for military use.

"What makes you think he was telling the truth?"

A fashion magazine editor is headed to a runway show when her cab collides with a hot dog stand.

139

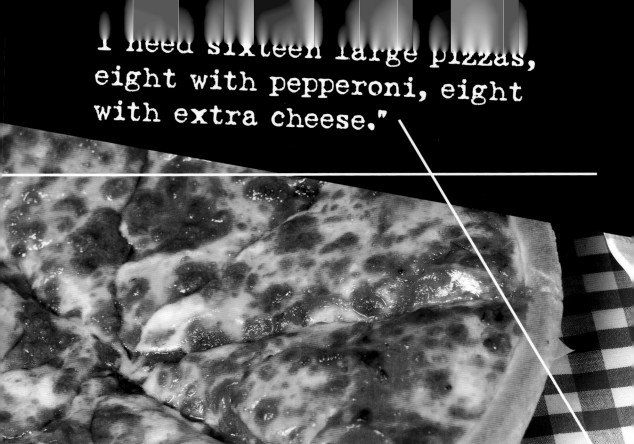

I need sixteen large pizzas, eight with pepperoni, eight with extra cheese."

A private investigator is hired to find out if a man's wife is cheating on him. What he discovers is far worse.

A young mother is faced with making a very tough decision regarding her emotionally unstable son.

"And then, of course, it jams."

Late one night, a woman has an epiphany that her life has been unfulfilling. What she really wants, however, is neither socially acceptable nor legal.

"I hope to God I never have to go through that."

A woman eating at a busy restaurant with her husband returns from the restroom to find that he has vanished. The waiter does not know where he went, or why.

Writing is the only thing that, when I do it, I don't feel I should be doing something else.
—Gloria Steinem

141

"Okay, I paid the twenty bucks. What do the cards say?"

A mother loses her temper and finally follows through on her oft-repeated promise to pull the car over and make the children walk home.

You are becoming increasingly uncomfortable with your boss's inappropriate behavior.

"Are you ever satisfied?"

A woman suspects that her husband is using their marriage and family as a cover for terrorist activities.

Two childhood friends reunite after twenty years. After several drinks, one of them admits to having murdered several people.

AN UNEMPLOYED WOMAN DECIDES TO PACK UP HER FOUR CATS AND MOVE TO A FOREIGN COUNTRY.

143

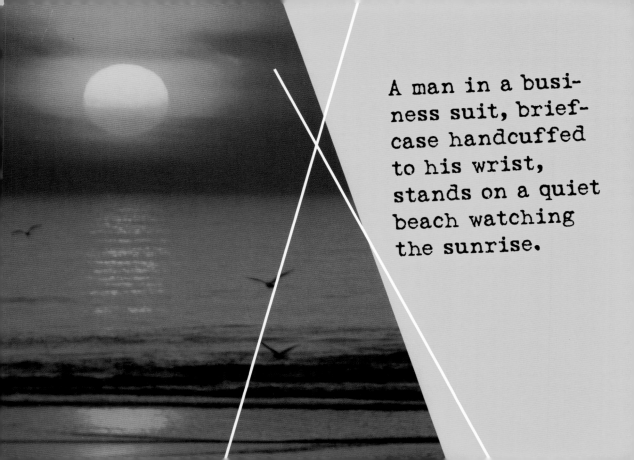

A man in a business suit, briefcase handcuffed to his wrist, stands on a quiet beach watching the sunrise.

A community learns that their homes were built on a newly discovered and potentially volatile fault line.

"Well, I don't know about you, but I like to know what I'm getting into."

A high school art teacher finds herself attracted to the father of one of her students.

"They say it's my liver."

An unstable, institutionalized woman believes herself to be a time traveler. She vows to escape to return to her own era.

A man receives a package in the mail from his brother who died seventeen years earlier.

"Yeah, she's got two kids, but so what?"

> You cannot write for children. ... They're much too complicated. You can only write books that are of interest to them.
> —Maurice Sendak

A married couple decides that they're finally ready for a family. After a year of trying to get pregnant, however, the woman's doctor informs them that she is unable to bear children.

Your friends insist that a waitress at your favorite diner has a crush on you.

A young woman with an eating disorder visits an all-you-can-eat restaurant with her co-workers.

"I love how she stretches every morning, like a cat."

"I'm going to disappoint you. But you knew that already."

A man worries that his employer is beginning to suspect he can't read.

A woman dreams of being in a car accident. The next day, she is. Then she dreams of winning free movie tickets. The next day, she does. On the third night, she dreams of being murdered.

"None of that 'eye for an eye' bullshit. I just want him dead."

A couple notices that their handyman has been stealing things from their medicine cabinet.

A beloved celebrity can no longer live with the pain of a shameful secret.

While surfing for porn on the Internet, a man comes across a picture of someone he knows.

"Every day I loved her, the claws went in a little bit deeper."

A scientist has an otherworldly experience, which forces him to reevaluate his spiritual beliefs.

The South won the Civil War. Consider how this outcome would have altered 21st-century America, then write a story from the point of view of the following contemporary characters:
- a young black man
- an older white woman of wealth and privilege
- a Japanese journalist in America

"You'll notice my wife doesn't drink."

A woman discovers that her boyfriend's apartment is heavily bugged.

"Hey, aren't you the pool man from the hotel?"

"He hates to fly. Hence the libations."

AN OLD MAN IS DINING ALONE IN A CROWDED RESTAURANT WHEN A FIRE BREAKS OUT.

149

A postal worker notices that the mailbox at one of his stops is overflowing, even though the family's two cars are in the driveway.

A child suspects that his father is putting something in his food to make him sick.

"How the hell can you be dying?"

After completely fabricating your résumé, you get a great new job for which you have no experience.

A family of squirrels discovers that the small forest in which they live is about to be destroyed to make room for a new housing project.

"Surprisingly, she's very low maintenance."

A journalist investigates a murder, only to discover that the clues point to her own son.

A cat decides to take action when its human companion fails to return home after several days.

"You've burned my waffles for the last time!"

"I've seen a lot, but I've got to admit, that freaks me out."

Three law enforcement officers are accused of police brutality. The person they are accused of having beaten disappears just before the Internal Affairs investigation begins.

"Grandpa, what does this crazy looking thing do?"

Writing is an exploration. You start from nothing and learn as you go.

—E. L. Doctorow

While plowing a newly purchased plot of land, a farmer discovers a mass grave.

An introverted young woman with no family is diagnosed with terminal cancer. She has only six weeks to live.

"Discretion is the better part of valor? What a load of crap."

An athlete is accused of using steroids. Although she believes herself to be innocent, the athlete's trainers have, in fact, been doping her with growth hormones.

A violinist loses a hand in a car accident.

"Look, the last thing I need is advice from a 'sanitation engineer.'"

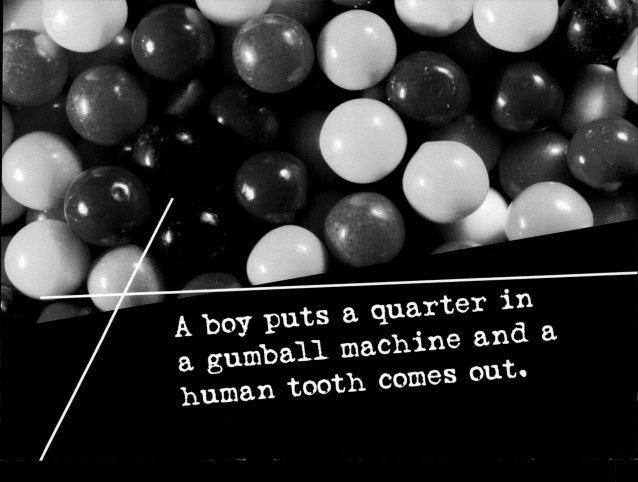

A boy puts a quarter in a gumball machine and a human tooth comes out.

"HELLO? HELLO? I THINK THE PHONE JUST WENT DEAD ..."

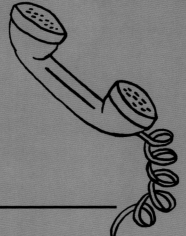

Believing herself immune to his powers of seduction, a young woman decides to confront the attractive lothario attempting to charm her sister.

"All right, all right, you can come over ... but only if you promise to behave."

A married woman attends a teamwork training retreat with several co-workers. Upon arriving, an attractive man from her office suggests that they have an affair.

After suffering a head injury, a father of five starts to believe that he is an animal.

A vocal cord nodule threatens the career of a well-known singer.

On his way to propose to his girlfriend, a man is approached on the subway by four youths.

"He might as well be dead to me now."

"Don't beat yourself up. This kind of thing could've happened to anyone."

A man claiming to be the world's greatest escape artist accepts the challenge to break out of a maximum-security prison within one week.

"That's it. Let's call it a night and get into some trouble."

A woman learns that one of her young daughters has used a home pregnancy test.

An elderly man decides to stop taking his medication.

The Chinese tradition of binding feet becomes fashionable among young women in the U.S.

A drug addict's only supplier is killed in a police raid.

A radio talk jock plans a farewell show as his station prepares to change to a soft rock format.

A woman buys a copy of her high school yearbook through an eBay auction.

An editorial cartoonist angers an aging, but powerful, politician.

On a whim, an inner-city high school senior buys a lottery ticket and wins thirty million dollars.

"You'd think that to look at her, but she's actually one of the smartest people I know."

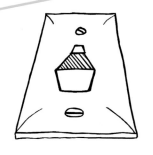

"Whatever you do, don't turn on the light. Please."

While researching a book on witchcraft, a writer accidentally witnesses a contemporary ritual involving a human sacrifice.

The son of a long-time soap opera diva goes on his first audition.

"You need special permission to view this material."

Venice, Italy is sinking rapidly and must be evacuated. As residents are fleeing, scientists, researchers, and others are arriving from around the world to record the extraordinary event. Write a related story from the viewpoint of the following protagonists:
- an art historian
- an American tourist
- a resident whose family has lived in Venice as far back as can be traced

"You've just slashed your last tire, *punk*."

A telemarketer begins to receive telephone threats from the customer she just called moments before.

A woman searching for a long lost love finds him in prison.

159

A man discovers that a lover has died of complications from AIDs.

"Somebody tell that to the walking shag carpet."

A reclusive young woman sets out to conquer her phobias.

A CIA operative discovers that the U.S. is about to be framed for a surprise attack upon a Middle-Eastern country in order to further destabilize the region.

I can't write five words but that I change seven.
—Dorothy Parker

"You wouldn't catch me dead wearing a get-up like that."

A professional wrestler discovers that his tag-team partner is taking a business course via the Internet.

"THAT IS THE BIGGEST BIRD
I HAVE EVER SEEN."

"Here she comes. I can hear her boots clunking up the stairs."

Two friends decide to ditch school for the day and explore the nearby sewer tunnels.

"Put that thing down, son."

A girl sets out to uncover the truth behind a local bakery's "top secret" cookie recipe.

A farmer finds a nest of strangely colored eggs in the middle of his cornfield.

A high school student finds a puzzling device inside the fetal pig he's dissecting in biology class.

After practicing his act for years, Leonard finally gets his big chance to audition for a television variety show.

A riot breaks out at a candlelight vigil for a dead rock star.

"Just where do you think you're going with that giraffe?"

"I'd be surprised if their marriage lasts a year."

A middle-aged insurance salesman begins sculpting clay figures on the weekend. Doing so, he finds, brings him great joy—so much so that he decides to quit his job.

"You are not going to believe what I found in his bathroom."

The owner of a large factory is informed by an EPA representative that he needs to install expensive, higher quality emission controls or shut down immediately.

"I know I've said it before, but this really is your last chance."

A woman slowly unravels after suffering a personal loss.

THREE WOMEN ARE EATING BREAKFAST TOGETHER AT A RESTAURANT WHEN ONE OF THEM BEGINS TO CHOKE ON SOMETHING.

A therapist at a battered women's shelter is beaten up by her boyfriend.

A garage band getting ready to record its first CD argues about changing the name of the band.

The owner of a drycleaner discovers something unusual in the coat pocket of one of his regular customers. Write about what happens when this discovery is:
- a plastic bag of illegal drugs
- a love letter
- a package of photos
- a treasure map

A marine biologist grows concerned when he discovers that fish near a government facility have begun to exhibit a particular deformity.

"Wouldn't *that* be romantic?"

The difference between the almost right word and the right word is ... the difference between the lightning-bug and the lightning.
—Mark Twain

"Abnormal psychology. What's your major?"

A young man of North African descent, but who has lived in the
United States almost his entire life, is deported back to the country
he never knew.

"I'm tired of all this waiting around. Let's beat it."

A man gets trapped in an elevator with
his ex-wife's "perfect" new boyfriend.

"I was expecting you to kiss me weeks ago."

Ugly becomes the new pretty, and women everywhere begin smoking,
eating too much dairy, and throwing away their moisturizers in an
attempt to achieve ultimate beauty.

Big tobacco announces that smoking increases penis size.

"She had the best calves I've ever seen."

A woman with a terrible disease is offered an experimental drug therapy.

In the middle of a blackout, a young college student is attacked in the offices of the psychology department.

"Don't look at me like that."

An illiterate man goes on a trip to China with his son's family, where, for the first time in his life, they have as hard a time getting by as he does.

"She lost the baby."

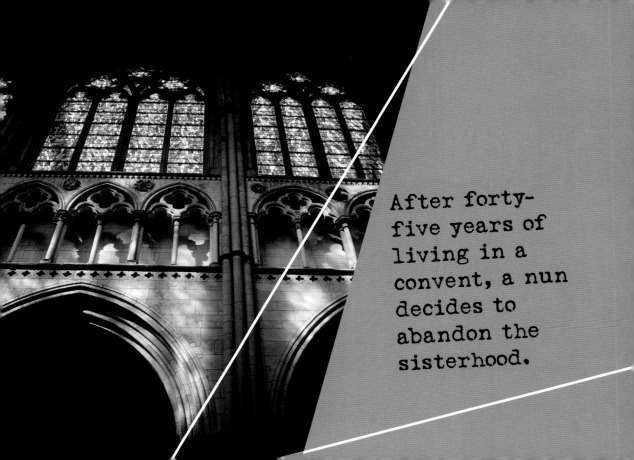

After forty-five years of living in a convent, a nun decides to abandon the sisterhood.

A FLORIDA GAME WARDEN VOLUNTEERS TO WORK UNDERCOVER TO APPREHEND MEMBERS OF AN ALLIGATOR-POACHING RING.

A woman receives an unlabeled video in the mail. On it, she finds her husband having sex with another woman. Just as the tape ends, he opens a drawer in their nightstand and pulls out a knife.

"It's not going to work out. I see that now."

People begin to exhibit strange abilities after visiting the local Indian ruins.

A couple renovating an old house discovers a secret passage.

"Can you *please* turn the camera off?"

The winner of a Tom Cruise look-alike contest moves to a small Midwestern town.

A dancer receives a recently blinded relative's ballet shoes.

"She just winked at me! Wait. Dude, did she wink at me?"

"Yeah, I'm bad. But in a good way."

Out of curiosity, a medical student attempts to reanimate her dead cat.

A brother and sister learn that their parents are planning to move the family out of the country.

"Are you here alone?"

A man arrives at an emergency room with a suspicious gunshot wound he claims was self-inflicted.

A vain woman takes prescription medication to treat an unsightly but harmless skin condition. The medication works, but at the expense of one of her vital organs.

I can shake off everything if I write; my sorrows disappear, my courage is reborn.
—Anne Frank

A radical hysterectomy is performed without the consent of the single woman in her early thirties who was admitted to the hospital with appendicitis.

"Can we dispense with the small talk and get down to business?"

A vagrant approaches a well-heeled man who exits a trendy coffee place with a five-dollar latte and a fat-free muffin.

A young boy lies in bed watching water slowly drip from the ceiling and cockroaches scurry across the threadbare apartment.

"You know you want to call him so why not do us all a favor and just get it over with."

A young woman with confidence issues slowly loses the only thing about herself that she loves—her long, beautiful hair.

Parents look on in horror as a magician's trick goes horribly awry during a child's birthday party.

An agoraphobic woman becomes obsessed with infomercials.

"It's supposed to be a game, but he treats it like life and death."

An elderly woman gets separated from her family while traveling from Los Angeles to Las Vegas.

A high school quarterback is offered a college scholarship, but only if he throws the state championship.

A couple comes home from vacation and finds their front door slightly ajar.

"Imagine that—a whole barrel full. This must be my lucky day!"

A woman is hired to be the private massage therapist for an unusual client. Write about her first session with:
- the president of the United States
- the lead singer of a rock band
- a spoiled socialite
- an eccentric billionaire
- a young man with a terminal illness

Immediately after bilking an old couple out of their savings, a con man stops by his son's elementary school for Career Day.

"You don't scare me, you poor excuse for a security guard."

A man's lover leaves him for someone else, but he doesn't know why.

A young couple is honeymooning in Hawaii when they bump into a man who claims to be the woman's estranged husband.

A retired geneticist receives a telephone call from the government asking him to help develop an army of clones.

"What would your wife say if she knew you were here?"

A woman is taken aback when she finds out that a man she's been flirting with has the same name as her ex-husband.

After suffering through several years of abuse as a child, a woman cannot tolerate intimate contact with another person—even though she desires it more than anything else.

A man pays a large sum of money to a stripper. The woman later overdoses on an expensive drug and may die. Upon returning to the club, the man is notified of her condition.

"This is University Hospital calling."

"I've got to get out of these clothes, fast."

"I feel like everything I say is being weighed and measured. It's unsettling."

A woman receives a letter from a convicted felon who claims to be the child she gave up for adoption twenty-five years earlier.

"So what exactly is going on here anyway?"

You put a rented DVD into your machine and hit "play." Instead of the expected menu, a man in white appears, tells you a potentially life-altering secret, then disappears from the screen.

"That was my great-grandmother's!"

At a summer camp reunion, an aging man's love for his long-dead childhood girlfriend is rekindled.

After learning to play chess during his incarceration, a rehabilitated felon sets out to join the U.S. Olympic team.

An illegal immigrant makes it into town and gets a job at the only hotel in the county.

A shepherd calls the local priest when one of his sheep gives birth to a lamb with seven eyes.

"You treat me like I'm expendable."

Two old friends reconnect via e-mail four years after one of them married and moved away.

A nosy man eavesdrops on his co-workers and immediately regrets what he hears.

After courting online for months, a couple finally meets face-to-face in a hotel bar. Neither looks anything like the pictures they exchanged.

"Twenty-seven hours of labor and *then* they decide she needs a C-section!"

A small-town factory owner is faced with the choice of laying off employees or closing the company's day care center.

"*That* will come back to haunt you."

You and the three other men in your apartment building make a bet to see who can seduce the newest tenant—an attractive single woman—first.

"There are at least fifty pounds of meat in the van."

A politician decides to retire and write a tell-all book about how Washington really works—but exposing some of what he knows could get him killed.

Two boys who have never met before discover that they can converse telepathically.

A young woman's husband dies suddenly. When the will is read, it's discovered that he left everything to someone she's never heard of.

"Being around you people makes me feel like a genius."

In the middle of a highly regarded play, one of the main actors has a mild stroke on stage and can't remember any of his lines.

Soon after hitting puberty, a young woman discovers that she can "see" when people are lying.

"About you? I'd have to say the little place right behind your earlobe."

At the age of eighteen, a young man buys a one-way ticket to India.

A man hears a loud pop as he walks through a busy intersection. Several minutes later he realizes that he's bleeding from the head.

"You want me to believe in God? Fine. I believe he's one twisted SOB."

A devout Christian is forced to lie to his family when he agrees to help the CIA.

Desperate for some fast cash, a college student volunteers to be a test subject for a company developing teleportation technology.

An ailing man and his wife consider assisted suicide.

"He makes me laugh. Most days, that's enough."

A RECEPTIONIST AT A DENTIST'S OFFICE ANSWERS THE TELEPHONE. THE VOICE AT THE OTHER END IS YELLING FOR HELP.

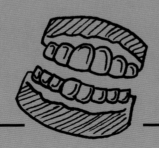

A man takes the train home from work to tell his wife of their financial ruin.

"Does anyone here have a reason why these two should not be married?"

After a violent thunderstorm, a man finds a rain-soaked diary among the debris in his yard.

"She thinks I *need* her. Can you believe it?"

A hungry young marketing professional is offered an extremely high-paying job. Unfortunately, it's in an industry that she finds repellent and immoral.

"Sir, I'm afraid you have to get off the plane."

A large family gathers for Thanksgiving dinner. As the patriarch carves the turkey, he casually announces that he and his wife of forty-eight years have decided to divorce.

"I'LL SEE YOUR SHOE, AND I'LL RAISE YOU ONE SOCK."

A man learns that what he thought was chronic heartburn is really terminal cancer.

Without warning, a massive earthquake hits Chicago. Write about the following people and what happens to them because of the quake:
- an emergency medical technician on her day off, at home in her 24th floor apartment
- a drug addict
- a retired father of four, riding his motorcycle through downtown traffic

A frazzled woman with two small children gets into an argument with a grocery store clerk.

Record-breaking floodwaters destroy a small farmer's entire crop.

"I guess we should try it. After all, it is the wine of the region."

A man witnesses an accident that kills his best friend.

A man who works at the World Trade Center calls in sick on September 11, 2001.

"Why does your boyfriend have a tuxedo in the back seat of his car?"

A woman's husband is pinned beneath their car after it skids off the road and flips over.

A ten-year-old boy suspects that his neighbor is wanted by the police.

"Danny, for God's sake, do not touch that!"

Nothing matters but the writing.
—Samuel Beckett

A man steals a large sum of money to cover a failed business deal. He gets away with the crime but is haunted by the nature of what he has done.

An undercover police officer discovers that her cover has been purposefully exposed by someone else on the force.

A racist man falls in love with a biracial woman.

"God, I hope I don't get picked last again."

A man waiting in a train station nervously checks his watch while pretending to read the paper.

"I pray everyday that it will stop, but it keeps getting worse."

A widower's legacy ends when his only son dies.

A woman falls passionately in love with her ex-husband.

A philosopher comes to the realization that all known existence is a product of his imagination.

A man discovers a large sum of money in his wallet and can't remember where it came from.

You run into an old friend from high school, who tells you an outrageous rumor about a former classmate.

A young man begins to realize that his life-long dream of starting his own breakfast cereal company will cost him everything and everyone he holds dear.

"The difference is that I lie for a reason!"

A homeless man artfully arranges trash on the sidewalk.

192

"The worst part of being a woman is the men."

Against his better judgment, a man decides to start dating a troubled, yet attractive, woman.

A man comes home to find that all of his trophies are missing from the mantle.

"Step into my office."

A sixteen-year-old girl sits alone in a clinic waiting for her test results.

An airline employee asks an obese passenger to pay for an extra seat.

A woman suffers a head injury that changes her personality. Now her husband must learn to adjust.

"Don't make this harder than it has to be ..."

When a crackpot inventor is killed by one of his own contraptions, his brother—also an inventor—finds himself compelled to finish the work.

"Which one do *you* like better?"

A street fair vendor serves contaminated food to hundreds of attendees. Write how it affects the following characters:
- a man, sick from the food, at the end of the bathroom line
- the cook
- the organizer of the fair

"So are you gonna kiss me or should I just call a cab?"

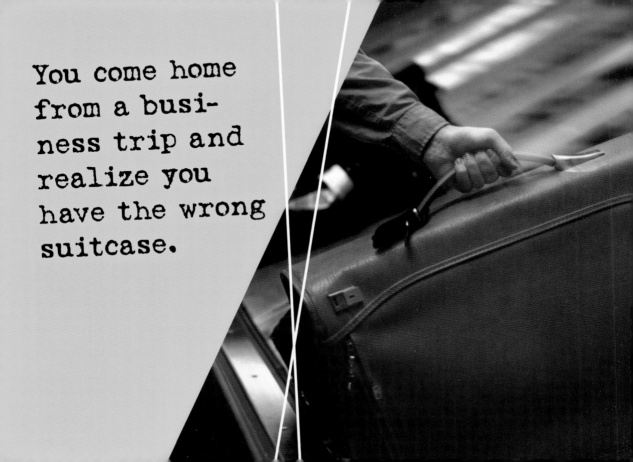

You come home from a busi- ness trip and realize you have the wrong suitcase.

A SINGLE, CELIBATE WOMAN IS TOLD THAT SHE IS PREGNANT.

Without warning, a waitress receives a wedding proposal from her favorite regular customer.

"You have been named as the legal guardian."

A woman goes to visit her mother at a nursing home. While there, her mother confesses that she wants to die and begs for her daughter's assistance.

"Tell me about the last time you saw him."

An elderly couple finds out that one of them has Alzheimer's disease.

"I don't think this was part of the deal."

A scientist leading an expedition into the Amazon is stung by an unusual-looking insect.

"Get ready to have your toes curled ..."

"It's lonely out here ... surrounded by all these people."

A life-long bigot changes his way of thinking after a single illuminating experience.

"Well, technically it's medicinal."

After studying French for two years, a woman takes a long-awaited trip to Paris.

"He stayed over last night."

A dairy worker develops the uncanny ability to communicate telepathically with livestock.

After his motorcycle breaks down, an American driving across the back roads of Europe has to hitchhike back to civilization.

"I don't think we can stop the bleeding."

I think all writing is a disease. You can't stop it.
—William Carlos Williams

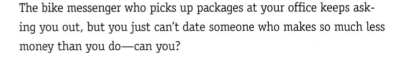
"I have come for my guitar."

The bike messenger who picks up packages at your office keeps asking you out, but you just can't date someone who makes so much less money than you do—can you?

"What if he says no?"

The CEO of a large corporation calls her staff together to make a surprising and life-altering announcement.

A scientist proves that God exists.

Everyday you walk through the park during your lunch break. And everyday you see the same woman sitting under the same tree with an open sketchbook. What she's sketching is unclear.

"You really got ripped off."

A little girl turns into an elephant.

Otherwise happily in love, a young newlywed must contend with her overbearing, interfering mother-in-law.

After waking from a coma, a woman discovers that she can smell fear.

"Please, don't!"

A young minister falls in love with a woman who doesn't believe in God.

"Passion. That's really what I miss."

After three weeks, a lost dog returns home to its master carrying an unidentifiable bone in its mouth.

A man, paralyzed for his entire adult life, suddenly regains the use of his right arm.

"So, where you from?"

For their honeymoon, a newlywed couple decides to go on a five-day photo safari in Africa. Midway through the trip, their caravan is attacked by poachers.

You come across your mother's high school yearbook and one of the inscriptions changes your perception of her.

"Daddy, don't let go."

While on vacation overseas, an ornithologist stumbles across a creature previously believed to be extinct.

THREE COLLEGE BUDDIES SPEND THE SUMMER WORKING IN AN ALASKAN FISHERY. THE CONSTANT DAYLIGHT BEGINS TO AFFECT THEIR PERFORMANCE AND JUDGMENT.

Determined to create a living work of art, a plastic surgeon begins operating on himself.

"Would you like me to tell you exactly what's wrong with you?"

"I don't know ... something about that guy creeps me out."

A woman suffering from insomnia and desperate for company, drives around looking for someplace—any place, really—that's open twenty-four hours.

A classic is a book that has never finished saying what it has to say.

—Italo Calvino

"I miss the warmth of her body the most."

A small-town baker becomes obsessed with baking the world's largest loaf of bread.

"What's that noise?"

A man on a bus notices a woman coughing up blood into a handkerchief.

"Um ... why don't you try taking the wrapper off first?"

Using the camera in her cell phone, a high school senior plots to get revenge on the students who made her life a living hell.

A young woman gets a chance to be on television, but the experience ends in complete humiliation.

A racist professor can't believe that his best student is an African-American woman.

205

A Mexican family decides to sneak into the United States to live and find work.

"I'm afraid that I have some bad news."

A woman decides to join the Peace Corps after her husband dies.

A teenage girl browsing at a department store notices a wealthy-looking woman casually shove merchandise into her purse.

A businessman is pulled over for a routine driving infraction but is arrested when the officer provokes him into taking a swing.

"I'm sorry. The odds against conception are very high."

The captain of a charter boat is hired to sail through the Bermuda Triangle

A PIECE OF A FALLEN SATELLITE CRASHES INTO THE BACKYARD OF A SMALL-TOWN FAMILY.

"I can't protect you from that."

Sudden fame puts a strain on the relationship of a young actress and her fiancé, a high school English teacher.

"I can't stress enough how lucky I am to have you kids."

A wanted felon is shot and left for dead by two of his associates.

A twenty-something man must speak with his parents. He sits in a taxi in front of their house, trying to find the courage to tell them that he:
- is gay
- killed someone in a drunk driving accident
- is moving overseas
- has been diagnosed with cancer
- got his girlfriend pregnant

A scientist discovers how to stop the aging process.

209

On a dare, a teenage girl sneaks into an abandoned house.

"Relax, would ya?"

A man is surprised to find himself feeling both pleased and liberated by the news that he will soon die.

"You're being deliberately obtuse."

In a crowded airport, a woman runs into her first—and greatest— love, whom she hasn't seen in decades.

"Hold her close and never let go, my man!"

In the aftermath of a tragic bumper-car accident, a young artist must regain her ability to draw—using her feet.

The best emotions to write out of are anger and fear or dread. ...

—Susan Sontag

"You know what, there's no point to this."

Seventeen years after making a pact that "if we're still single when we're forty, we'll marry each other," two friends head downtown to buy a marriage license.

"Honestly, now. What do you think of her?"

A man begins to have a recurring dream about a woman he does not know.

A woman undergoes cosmetic eye surgery that most doctors deem "safe." A few years later, however, she begins to go blind.

Returning home well after curfew, a teenage boy finds that his parents are nowhere to be found. What's even stranger is the giant inflatable monkey standing in the yard.

A chance encounter exposes the criminal practices of a well-known doctor.

While filling up her car with gas, a woman finds the words "help me" and a license plate number written in lipstick on her passenger door.

"Any minute now. ..."

A hermit in a log cabin in the woods hears an unexpected knock at the door.

"If you love me, you'll eat this."

A man must reevaluate his ideas about beauty when his wife is disfigured in an accident.

After having participated in a plastic surgery reality television show, a woman heads off to her class reunion.

"I think Mom is psychic."

A man takes lunch to his wife's office, and he's told that she hasn't worked there in weeks.

"Well, he was a good man while he lasted."

A young reporter is given an opportunity to cover the mistreatment of refugees in a war-torn African nation. The assignment is quite dangerous, but the reporter knows that such a story could make or break her career.

After supporting the tobacco industry for years, the president of the United States develops lung cancer.

A MAN OPENS HIS MAILBOX TO FIND
AN ENVELOPE CONTAINING A SET
OF INSTRUCTIONS.

You discover what looks to be a famous painting in your grandmother's attic. Upon further investigation, you learn that it's a stolen masterpiece.

"I wasn't trying to stare. It's just that ... well ... she's beautiful, don't you think?"

A waiter at a neighborhood diner begins to have prophetic dreams about his regulars.

"Is this the master key?"

A recovering addict finds a fifty-dollar bill while walking to his twelve-step meeting.

When a man regains consciousness, he finds he's been tarred and feathered.

216

"I want my money back."

With nothing left to lose, a washed up prizefighter begins stalking
the current world champion, intent on challenging the man to a
street fight.

You run into your ex-lover in the checkout line
at the drug store. You're buying condoms; he's
buying diapers.

"We can't let this continue."

After giving away an extremely large sum of money to charity, a
wealthy man's investments go belly up.

An elderly couple finds a bottle of Viagra.

"My sister is off limits, got it?"

A surfer goes to the beach one morning to find that the ocean has turned blood red.

"Somebody's got to stop him."

At the Academy Awards, a vain, egotistical actor at the end of his career contemplates suicide after losing what is likely to be his final opportunity to win an Oscar.

"I had three kids. Two boys and a girl."

After a night of heavy drinking, a teenager accidentally slams into another car. Although no one is killed, the teenager's best friend is paralyzed from the waist down.

A youth is invited by his best friend to attend a snake-handling church service.

"So who's the
idiot stuck in
the elevator?"

AN AWKWARD, NERDY TEEN DEVISES AN ELABORATE SCHEME TO GAIN POPULARITY.

A woman who suspects her husband of cheating decides to get revenge by cheating on him.

"Forgive me, Father, for I have sinned. A lot."

A writer famous for her horror stories composes a tale that grows so terrifying she's too afraid to complete it—much to the chagrin of her agent.

"Do what I tell you and everything will be just fine."

A bodyguard freezes at a critical moment, allowing the person under his protection to be killed.

At the reading of their father's will, a group of estranged siblings are provided with a string of clues leading to a buried treasure, one clue for each sibling.

For me, writing something down was the only road out.
—Anne Tyler

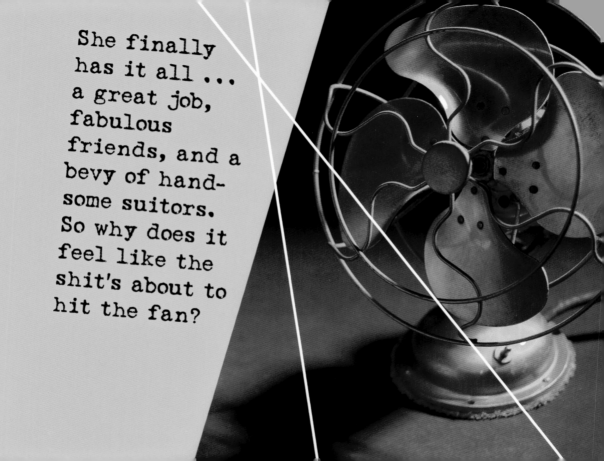

She finally has it all ... a great job, fabulous friends, and a bevy of hand-some suitors. So why does it feel like the shit's about to hit the fan?

While eating at the counter of a busy diner, a deaf man reads the lips of a fry cook who's telling a co-worker about the broken glass he folded into the omelet of a belligerent customer.

"Would you please put us out of your misery and go talk to her already?"

While snooping around her daughter's computer, a mother finds that the girl has been chatting online with a much older man.

A woman on her honeymoon is shocked to hear a secret from her husband's past.

"It's weird, I know, but I kind of *like* going to the doctor's."

A battered wife sees an opportunity to leave her husband when he is hospitalized due to a heart attack.

"Dad is dying."

While walking down the street, a young girl spots a glowing pair of eyes peering out from a sewer drain.

"My God, this is like that old Abbott and Costello routine, 'Who's on First?'"

You run into your favorite high school teacher sitting alone at a bar, his only company a glass of whiskey. He invites you to sit down and tell him about your life.

"Patience. It was her name. It was her gift. At least when it came to me, it was."

An unhappy customer harasses employees at a mail-order food business.

An attractive young woman flirts with a cute guy in a crowded gym. As she stops to stretch, she involuntarily emits a loud, rude noise.

"I want you back. Why is that?"

A blind woman's guide dog begins speaking to her when they are alone.

While on a long overseas flight, a young businessman in the midst of a spiritual crisis finds himself seated next to a well-known religious leader.

A woman discovers that her new boyfriend is also a white supremacist.

"Why, hello Billy! Let's go save the universe, shall we?"

A young girl finds a secret panel at the back of her closet that leads to another world.

"A haunted what?"

A woman contemplating suicide visits a psychic.

"I'm Jewish. Deal with it."

A young man falls in love with a successful older woman who doesn't know he exists.

Due to critical paper shortages, all books must be published as electronic documents. Printing books on paper is illegal. Write about how the following people cope:

- a librarian whose books have now become collector's items
- the leader of an underground movement known as "retro readers"
- a blind man whose window to the world was Braille

"It's quiet. Somehow that makes me sad."

A new employee discovers that his co-workers worship the devil.

226

A WOMAN UNDERGOES GASTRIC BYPASS SURGERY AND CANNOT STOP LOSING WEIGHT.

227

"Do me a favor, would you? Dumb it down."

A one-armed woman gets a job as a hotel maid.

Something bizarre occurs at the table next to a couple on their first date.

Two friends return from an around-the-world-tour only to discover that they've been pronounced dead.

"I don't care what anybody says, *these* are the glory days."

While on a camping trip, a couple sees what they think is a UFO. After returning home, the wife discovers that she is pregnant.

Random items are slowly disappearing from a single man's apartment.

After incorrectly installing airbags in twenty vehicles, a factory worker realizes his mistake and knows it could cost him his job if discovered.

"You act like your life is a *Monty Python* skit."

A young man gets a call that his estranged parents have been in a car accident.

"Back in line, Williams."

While working in the garden, a young mother notices that her little boy is about to step on a snake.

While conducting an autopsy on a young man who died under suspicious circumstances, a coroner discovers that one of the man's teeth is hollow and hides something unusual inside.

"You've been watching too many movies, my friend."

It is a delicious thing to write, whether well or badly …

—Gustave Flaubert

Two adult siblings find themselves attracted to the same
person at a wedding.

While on a weekend excursion, a group of hikers notice a parasite in their water filtration system.

"At the end of the day, I expect to look back on this as a minor setback."

A young man working in social services finds his own records in the archives.

Recently divorced—and still stinging from the experience—a young woman composes her personal profile for a singles Web site.

After working together for several weeks, you start to generate unexpected sparks with the foreign exchange student you're tutoring.

"I tried killing her with kindness, but it didn't work."

"And that's when I quit."

A woman humiliates herself during a company party and fears returning to work.

A child makes a shocking discovery while digging around at the local dump.

While being nursed back to health in New Orleans, the victim of a terrible motorcycle accident gains super powers from drinking his father's special herbal tonic.

Writing and reading is to me synonymous with existing.
—Gertrude Stein

"Your father hates me, doesn't he?"

A child develops an overwhelming fear that everyone he loves will soon die violently.

"Funny how your eyes always look away when you say that."

"Come with or stay at home. It's your misery."

After falling asleep on a twenty-hour bus ride to his mother's house, a college student wakes up to discover that he's been on the wrong bus the entire time.

Months after receiving a gunshot wound to the head, a patient is discharged from the hospital. She wears a pendant made from the bullet that was imbedded in her skull.

A woman is raped by her husband.

"He's attractive, he's funny, he's rich. Why am I not interested?"

The day before helping her best friend give birth, a woman of thirty learns that she will never have children of her own.

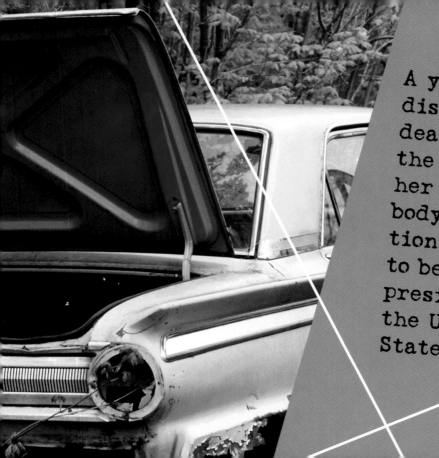

A young woman discovers a dead body in the trunk of her car. The body in question appears to be the president of the United States.

A COMPANY REPRESENTATIVE RETURNS FROM A SALES TRIP CLAIMING TO HAVE MET THE DEVIL.

Ben Jackson, husband and father of three, is killed in a car accident. Write about this event and how it affects the lives of the following characters:

- Ben's wife
- Ben's business partner
- a police officer who was at the scene of the accident
- Ben's youngest child

"Let's just agree that we both hate her, okay?"

A deaf woman undergoes a surgical procedure that enables her to hear for the first time.

"He makes films. I didn't ask what kind."

Unexpectedly, the U.S. government outlaws smoking, with very little resistance from the tobacco industry.

... writing is not a performance but a generosity.
—Brenda Ueland

While at a family reunion, a teenage brother and sister find an old suitcase filled with money under their uncle's bed.

"I think I survived pretty good, actually. You should see everybody else."

An army private learns that he has to go back to war for a second tour.

The figure in a famous painting begins communicating with an art museum patron.

A couple of goth high school students get busted for shoplifting and are sentenced to do community service with Habitat for Humanity.

A police detective is assigned to a case involving arson at several Krispy Kreme donut shops.

"Weird little things remind me of her. I don't even know why. Cabbage, for instance."

A man comes to believe that he is an emissary of God when he survives a plane crash in which all other passengers are killed.

"I ... love you?"

A lawyer discovers that his client is guilty of the horrible crime for which he was just found innocent.

"I love the way she says words that begin with 'cr', like 'crisp' and 'crunchy'. How bizarre is that?"

A con man starts to admire the achievements of the man he is impersonating.

A MOTHER DISCOVERS A FEMININE COLLECTION WHILE CLEANING HER SON'S BEDROOM.

An elderly couple disagrees about what to do with their sick house cat.

"Lucky you, I'm free tonight. One show only, though, okay?"

A man sneezes painfully. He looks in his handkerchief and finds something that looks like a microchip.

"Yes, and *that's* when she broke the plate over his head!"

The owner of a puppet theater goes on a crime spree with an inanimate accomplice.

An air force pilot is ordered to destroy a public building in a major metropolitan city.

"Let go.
You can
trust me."

While relaxing on his porch swing, a pig farmer hears a tremendous crash in a nearby field.

A woman gets the opportunity of a lifetime when she gets hired to sing backup for a famous musician.

"I rubbed my thumb across her cheek and, buddy, I thought I was going to cry."

A man traveling overseas meets the woman of his dreams, but they don't speak a common language.

Four men decide to rob a bank. Two of the men intend to take all of the money, even if it means killing their partners.

A young mother is told that her children have been killed in a drive-by shooting.

You inadvertently run an important paper through the shredder.

APPENDIX 1

GET MORE OUT OF YOUR PROMPTS

If you use one prompt a day, this book will last you almost three years. We assume, of course, that you'll want to get even more use out of it than that. To that end, we've provided a number of suggestions for varying your prompts, making each one an interesting new challenge every time you use it.

VARIATION TABLES

On the surface, the variations detailed on the next few pages may seem obvious. They are. But consider this: writers tend to follow the path of least resistance. If you like mysteries, you'll gravitate toward prompts that easily conform to the standards of that genre. If you like third-person point of view, that's what you'll tend to write, time and again. And in general fiction, you're probably most comfortable writing about characters like yourself, in terms of age, race, and sex. Use the variations below to break those unfortunate habits and stretch your writing muscles.

You can use the variation tables that follow in two ways:

1. Pick a prompt—situation, dialogue, or *one* assignment option. Select a variation that you wouldn't normally consider from one of the tables. Apply this variation to the prompt and start writing.

2. Pick a prompt. Select a variation table. Roll one six-sided die to determine the variation you *must* adhere to while writing the prompt. Using two tables is more fun. If you're feeling bold, roll against three tables. Daredevils might try four. (Five or six is madness—don't try it unless you're a trained professional.) If a randomly selected variation matches your usual approach to writing, or the original criteria of the prompt, re-roll.

TABLE A	
Number:	Your protagonist is:
1–3	Female
4–6	Male

TABLE B	
Number:	Your protagonist is:
1	< 18 years old
2	18–30 years old
3	31–50 years old
4	51–70 years old
5	> 70 years old
6	Re-roll

TABLE C	
Number:	Your protagonist is:
1	European or of European descent
2	African or of African descent
3	Latin or of Latin descent
4	Asian or of Asian descent
5	Native American or of Native American descent
6	Other

TABLE D	
Number:	The genre is:
1	Mystery/Thriller
2	Literary
3	Science Fiction/Fantasy
4	Horror
5	Romance
6	Humor

TABLE E	
Number:	The time period is:
1	Now
2	1 to 25 years in the future
3	25 to 500 years in the future
4	Late 20th century (1951–2000)
5	Early 20th century (1900–1950)
6	100 to 10,000 years ago

TABLE F	
Number:	The point of view is:
1–2	1st person
3–4	3rd person
5–6	Omniscient

In the case of Table E, you may have to make additional modifications to your chosen prompt. For example, if the prompt requires that a car be part of the story, and you've rolled a 6 on the table above, you may want to make the vehicle in question a horse or wagon.

VARIATIONS SPECIFIC TO SITUATION PROMPTS

Here's another fun tactic. Pick a situation prompt. Now write the prompt from the point of view of a character other than the obvious protagonist. For example, in the following prompt, you would most likely assign "man" the role of protagonist:

> A man who believes that his daughter's career is keeping her from getting married decides to take matters into his own hands.

Instead of going that route, write the prompt from the point of view of the daughter whose father constantly undermines her attempts at getting ahead. Or tell the story using a character we haven't even specified, such as the daughter's exasperated boyfriend, or her outraged mother.

APPENDIX 2

USING PROMPTS IN WRITING GROUPS

The editors at *Fresh Boiled Peanuts* love writing groups. Many of us have belonged to a writing group, at one time or another, and found the experience invaluable. One of the problems writing groups have, however, is ensuring that there's something interesting to do every time they meet. If stories haven't been turned in for discussion, or if previously submitted stories haven't been read, apathy and disappointment are the likely result. Bottom line: If your group has nothing to do, people will stop coming. That's where prompts can add to the fun.

Prompts can be a regular part of your meetings, or the saving grace of a meeting gone bad. They're fun, and they don't have to take up a great deal of time. Give each member a different prompt and start writing. After a set period of time (no more than, say, thirty minutes), stop and let each member of the group read what they have written. Don't expect perfection. Instead, listen for choice bits of dialogue, description, or characterization. Enjoy one another's efforts and discuss if anything further can be done with the work.

A variation on this exercise is to assign the *same* prompt to all group members. Spend your thirty minutes writing and then compare stories. The different ways in which people extrapolate on the same basic information is fascinating. And bouncing such ideas off of one another can be inspiring and energizing.

Finally, consider assigning prompts at the end of your writing group session. A different prompt for each member, or the same, it doesn't matter. The next time you meet you'll have longer pieces to discuss, even if only a few members contribute.

SUGGESTED READING

Baty, Chris. *No Plot? No Problem!* San Francisco: Chronicle Books, 2004.

Edgerton, Les. *Finding Your Voice*. Cincinnati, Ohio: Writer's Digest Books, 2003.

Frey, James N. *The Key*. New York: St. Martin's Press, 2000.

Glatzer, Jenna. *Outwitting Writer's Block and Other Problems of the Pen*. Guilford, Connecticut: The Lyons Press, 2003.

Goldberg, Natalie. *Writing Down the Bones*. Boston: Shambhala, 1986.

Goldsberry, Steven Taylor. *The Writer's Book of Wisdom*. Cincinnati, Ohio: Writer's Digest Books, 2005.

Heffron, Jack. *The Writer's Idea Book*. Cincinnati, Ohio: Writer's Digest Books, 2000.

Heffron, Jack. *The Writer's Idea Workshop*. Cincinnati, Ohio: Writer's Digest Books, 2003.

King, Stephen. *On Writing: A Memoir of the Craft*. New York: Scribner, 2000.

Lamott, Anne. *Bird by Bird*. New York: Anchor Books, 1995.

Lukeman, Noah. *The Plot Thickens*. New York: St. Martin's Press, 2002.

Masello, Robert. *Robert's Rules of Writing*. Cincinnati, Ohio: Writer's Digest Books, 2005.

Morrell, David. *Lessons from a Lifetime of Writing*. Cincinnati, Ohio: Writer's Digest Books, 2002.

Sellers, Heather. *Page after Page*. Cincinnati, Ohio: Writer's Digest Books, 2004.

Tobias, Ronald B. *20 Master Plots (and How to Build Them)*. Cincinnati, Ohio: Writer's Digest Books, 1993.

Wiesner, Karen. *First Draft in 30 Days*. Cincinnati, Ohio: Writer's Digest Books, 2005.

Wood, Monica. *The Pocket Muse: Ideas and Inspiration for Writing*. Cincinnati, Ohio: Writer's Digest Books, 2002.

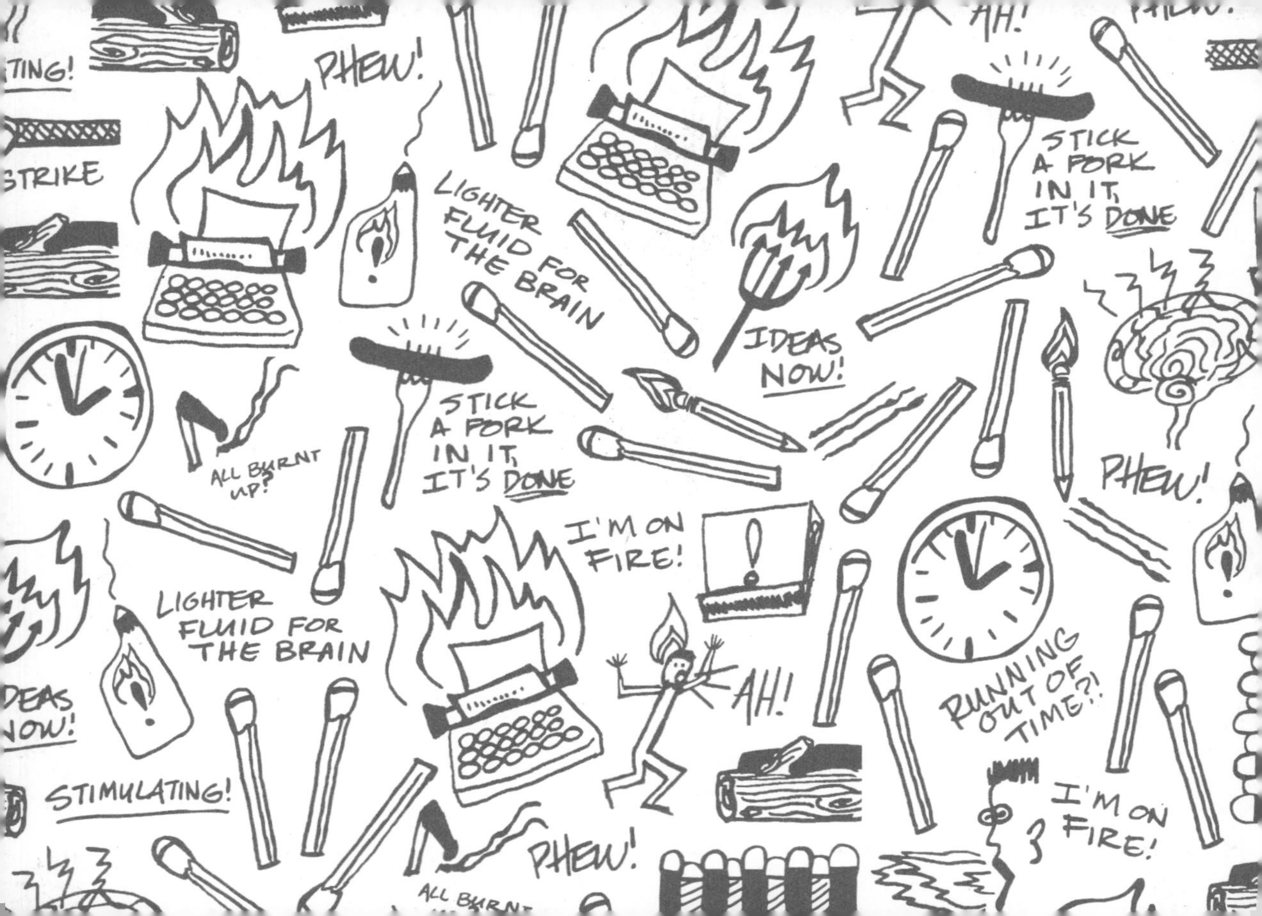